CATALOGUE OF THE
AKSUMITE COINS
IN THE BRITISH MUSEUM

CATALOGUE OF THE
AKSUMITE COINS
IN THE BRITISH MUSEUM

STUART MUNRO-HAY

Published for The Trustees of The British Museum by BRITISH MUSEUM PRESS

© 1999 The Trustees of the British Museum
Published by British Museum Press
A division of The British Museum Company Ltd
46 Bloomsbury Street, London WC1B 3QQ

British Library Cataloguing in Publication Data
A catalogue record for this book is available from the British Library

ISBN 0-7141-0883-9

Designed by Harry Green

Printed in Great Britain

Contents

Preface

In preparing this catalogue of the holdings of Aksumite coins in the Department of Coins and Medals at the British Museum, the opportunity has also been taken to update the account of Aksumite coin types by including new discoveries since the publication of my previous work *The Coinage of Aksum* in 1984.

Since that publication, a number of new types of Aksumite coins have appeared. In addition, the large and very important al-Madhariba hoard found in the Yemen has been studied and published (Munro-Hay 1989ii). The new evidence has not only filled out the series, but studies of die-links and other features have provided further clues towards the reconstruction of Aksumite chronology, an element of Aksumite studies to which the coins still remain the most important key. The order of kings in this catalogue thus differs from that in the former book, profiting from the new information. For a revision of the 1984 book, see Munro-Hay and Juel-Jensen 1995.

In this catalogue of the British Museum collection, all types of Aksumite coins known to date have been included, supplementing *The Coinage of Aksum*. Also, photographs have been used for illustrations where possible, again supplementing the type drawings used in the previous book. For coins lacking in the British Museum collection – which has recently become a more generally representative one, particularly strong in the silver issues, by the addition of the Brereton collection (Carradice 1989), though still rather lacking in gold – coins from other sources, in particular the exceptional collection belonging to Dr B. Juel-Jensen, have been illustrated. But a number of types remain without a photograph. The Juel-Jensen pieces, like the British Museum ones, are all enlarged (approximately × 2), and appear on separate plates under their (J-J) numbers. A unique coin of Wazeba in the Bibliothèque Nationale, Paris, likewise appears under its BN number.

The numbering system for the different types of Aksumite coin has also been revised, employing, instead of the former designations by metal, AV, AR, AE, a simple running numerical sequence. This need not be immediately outdated by the next new discovery, since the system can be continuously extended by use of letters and roman numerals for new types. I have not always been completely consistent. Sometimes, where a basic type seems to have numerous very minor variants in lettering or some other element, these are simply noted as variants in the main type, but on other occasions, usually in the case of much rarer types, a variant may have a separate numerical designation. The photographs are not arranged to show the die-axis of the coins; this is noted separately in the catalogue, except in the case of those issues where there was evidently no attempt at all to align the dies.

During the preparation of this catalogue I have received much help from members of staff of the Department of Coins and Medals, particularly from the Keeper, Andrew Burnett, and from Elizabeth Savage, Venetia Porter and Joe Cribb. Outside the Museum, Dr Bent Juel-Jensen has, as so often before, assisted me in every way possible, with access to his collection and use of his photographs, not to mention early information about new discoveries and scientific work, and the pleasure of discussion. I am very grateful to him, and also to M. Michel Amandry of the Cabinet des Médailles of the Bibliothèque Nationale, Paris, for photographs and information.

I am also grateful to the Lowick Fund of the Royal Numismatic Society for a grant to help me complete the catalogue. Working independently of any funding institutions, and outside England, this aspect too has its importance.

STUART MUNRO-HAY

Introduction

The east African highland state of Aksum, centred on its capital in the modern province of Tigray in Ethiopia, for several centuries issued a coinage – an exceptional feature in the Africa of its day. The coinage seems to have been produced from the end – perhaps the last quarter – of the third century AD to about the end of the first quarter of the seventh century. No other sub-Saharan African state issued its own independent coinage in ancient times. Indeed, only a few other contemporary states anywhere in the world could issue coinage in gold, a statement of sovereignty only achieved at the time of Aksum's power by Rome, Persia – to a lesser degree – and the Kushan kingdom in northern India and Afghanistan. Coins of Rome have been found in several places in Aksumite Ethiopia and Aksum-dominated southern Arabia, dating from the time of the Antonines to Theodosius II. Coins of the Kushan kings Vima Kadphises II, Kanishka, Huviska and Vasudeva, dated from *c.* AD 80 to 200 (or considerably later by some students of the series: see W. R. O. Hahn's review of Munro-Hay 1991 in the *Numismatic Chronicle*, 1993, p. 317), came from a find at the monastery of Debra Damo.

The simple fact of Aksum's coin production over an extended period is an indication of the way in which the culture and economy of the Aksumite state had developed. This coinage is also the only preserved medium, apart from some categories of archaeological finds such as pottery, through which we can observe some of the artistic trends current in Aksum at the time.

Aksum commenced its coin issues at a moment when trade links with the Roman world through Egypt, with the southern Arabian kingdom, and with parts of India and Sri Lanka had doubtless made it seem worthwhile to the kings to issue their own coinage. This would have replaced the imported foreign coinage which, together with 'pieces of cut brass to serve as coinage', appears from information given in a mid-first-century guide-book to Red Sea/Indian Ocean trade, the *Periplus of the Erythraean Sea* (Huntingford 1980, Casson 1989), to have been used previously by foreign merchants at Aksum's port of Adulis. From this period onwards Aksum was a powerful partner in the Red Sea/Indian Ocean commercial network, with at times considerable territorial interests in the Yemeni coastlands and even highlands as well. A few (pre-coinage) Aksumite kings are mentioned in inscriptions there, and King

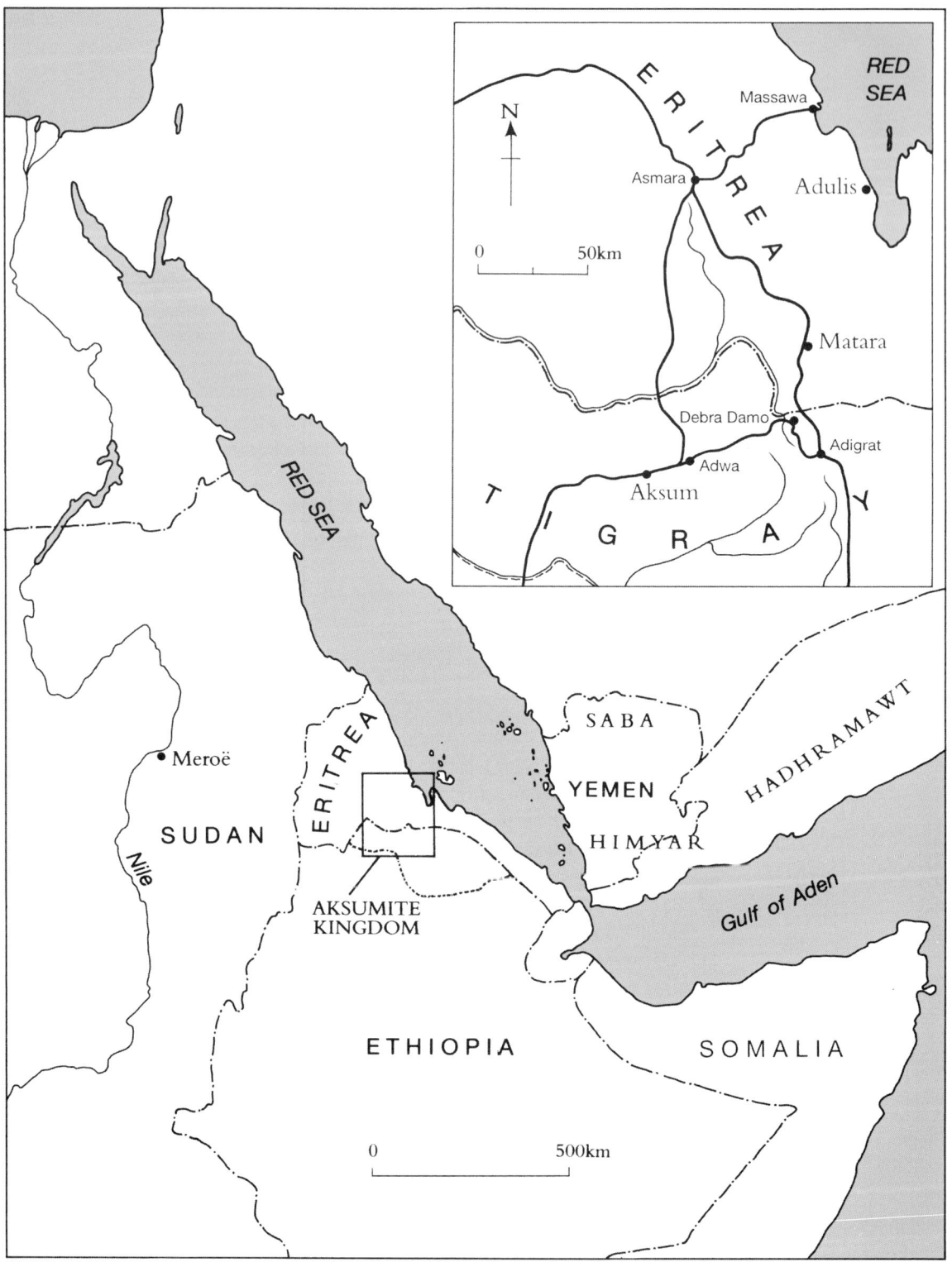

Ezana claimed the title of ruler of the Arabian kingdoms of Saba and Himyar (see Munro-Hay 1991, ch. 4, for an account of this period). Other Aksumite rulers would later add the title of king of Hadhramawt, the coastal plain and the Yemeni highlands with 'all their Arabs' as well.

In the Ethiopian highlands Aksumite power expanded too, the rulers adopting the title 'king of kings', *negusa nagast* in the Ethiopic (*Ge'ez*) language, to indicate their domination over certain subordinate groups. Even some Nubian peoples (Noba), the Beja and the Kushites or Kasu, were included in the extended titularies (on the few surviving inscriptions) of the Aksumite kings from the time of King Ezana in the mid-fourth century until the reigns of Kaleb and his son W'ZB in the mid-sixth century (Munro-Hay 1991, ch. 11, gives English translations of these, and see also Littmann 1913, Schneider 1974). The capital city of Aksum itself grew impressive. There were grandiose palaces, and avenues of stone commemorative thrones which probably bore some of the bilingual inscriptions, written in three scripts (Greek, Ge'ez and South Arabian), which have survived until today. Some of these mention gold, silver and bronze statues dedicated to the gods Mahrem, Beher, Meder and Astar. Most characteristic of all were the giant decorated stelae of granite – and their plainer precursors – which marked the royal necropolis. Some of the royal tombs were excavated by the British Institute in Eastern Africa (Munro-Hay 1989, 1991): work has now been resumed and may well produce more chronological information to assist with dating the Aksumite coinage.

The kings of Aksum struck coins of gold, silver and bronze. Issues in the two less valuable metals, uniquely, were sometimes overlaid with gold on certain important symbols like the royal head or later the cross or royal crown. The names of over twenty otherwise unknown kings of Aksum are preserved on this coinage, which thus constitutes a vital element in any attempt to reconstruct a chronological framework for Aksumite history. Fortunately, two kings named on the coinage, Ezana (mid-fourth century) and Kaleb (early sixth century), are also known from their own inscriptions (see above) and from some brief notes in the works of foreign authors, for example Patriarch Athanasius of Alexandria's *Apologia ad Constantium Imperatorem* (Szymusiak 1958), Procopius (Dewing 1914) and the *Letter* of Simeon of Beth Arsham (Shahid 1971, p. 63). These provide two fixed points in the sequence of this coinage. The Chronology below (p. 26) shows an approximate ordering of the kings based on such internal features of the coinage as weight, gold fineness, stylistic development and palaeography. We need to emphasise the word 'approximate': in spite of many efforts, gradually gaining precision as more coins become available and study of die-linkage, debasement, gold inlay techniques and other features increases, there are still many doubtful areas in the chronology of Aksumite coinage. Any new coin, or the discovery of more overstruck examples, might change our ideas about the sequence. Each new study brings more refinements. Many pieces, including some in the British Museum collection, remain the sole known examples of their particular type. Inevitably, under such circumstances, it is unrealistic to expect any sort of definitive ordering. Nevertheless, the broad outlines of the chronology seem now to be fairly firmly established.

During the existence of the Aksumite coinage – spanning the period from *c.* AD 270/290 to the seventh century when Aksum's power began to wane – the weight of the gold coins appears to have been closely linked with the contemporary Roman system. The heaviest Aksumite gold coins issued were equal to half the Roman aureus of the early fourth century. As the Roman system changed, so the Aksumite system followed, producing from Ezana's time gold coins of about 1.60g, representing the theoretical weight of 1.65g of the Roman 9-siliqua piece after Constantine the Great's monetary reforms. Later, *c.* 383, the Romans introduced a lighter tremissis of 1.50g, but Aksum remained with the heavier type, perhaps to offset another feature of the coinage – its debasement.

Although for a while there seems to have been an interest in maintaining a similar weight system, though often at a slightly lower level which may not simply indicate wear, the Aksumites failed to retain the purity of the gold which made Roman coinage so reliable (Oddy and Munro-Hay 1980; Munro-Hay, Oddy and Cowell 1988). The first kings issued coins of reasonably high gold content, but by the reign of Ezana in the mid-fourth century the percentage of gold had already fallen from the 90s to the 80s. It may have been awareness of this defect which caused the Aksumite ruler contemporary with the reform of Theodosius I, *c.* AD 383, not to follow the weight reduction to the true one-third solidus at about 1.50g, but to continue issuing at the previous weight. Fifth- and sixth-century rulers issued coins with percentages of gold sinking to the late 60s and 70s, Kaleb's lowest gold percentage recorded so far being 64.2 per cent. After him, the percentage levels for rulers like Ella Gabaz and Ioel fell as low as the early 50s. Two gold coins of Iathlia (probably a badly written Greek rendering of the royal name Ḥataz or Ḥataza known from the Ge'ez legends of his silver and bronze coinage) in Addis Ababa museum, unmeasured but optically inspected, are of a very pale gold which probably contains a heavy admixture of silver. This debasement, whilst at first profitable to the issuers, must eventually have struck a profound blow to the confidence of users, and may have contributed to the ending of the monetary system. The exact relation of the other metals to each other – complicated by the gold overlay on some types – or their relation to the gold, is unknown.

The symbolism adopted for the coinage was all-important in a world where such mobile items formed an excellent propaganda medium (Munro-Hay 1984iv). Endubis (Types 1–3), generally accepted as being the first king of Aksum to issue coins, established the basic outlines of style, which were followed fairly closely by his successors. The primary image was that of the king himself, an absolute ruler claiming divine affiliation (we know that a little later Ezana called himself 'Son of Mahrem', a god paralleled with the Greek war god Ares in his inscriptions). The kings from the time of Endubis' successor Aphilas (cf. Types 4–5) onwards can be seen on the obverse of the gold pieces wearing the elaborate Aksumite tiara, a high crown supported on a little colonnade of columns. Above their heads are the divine symbols, the disc and crescent. Since the kings used the epithet Son of Mahrem, perhaps it is this deity himself that these symbols represent. Or perhaps the whole Aksumite pantheon is symbolically invoked by them; sometimes several dots flank the main disc and crescent. The Christian cross succeeded to this predominant position on the coinage with the conversion of King Ezana, probably in the AD 330s, remaining with the figure of the king the chief iconographical feature until the end of the coinage.

The kings are draped, as the half-length profile busts from Aphilas' time onwards show, in robes, sometimes apparently fringed. The changes in the style of these draperies, and other items of regalia depicted on the coins, are sometimes a useful chronological indicator. Only Armaḥ (Types 152–3) is shown full-length (apart from the exceptional gold piece of MḤDYS, Type 67, recently discovered (Munro-Hay 1995), which also shows a full-length figure, in this instance wearing a baggy trouser-like garment). The kings are shown adorned with a considerable amount of jewellery; necklaces, bracelets, armlets and probably finger-rings. They hold a sword, a spear, a short stick (?), or a sceptre (?), and an object which may represent a fly-whisk; or later, in Christian times, a hand-cross. The bust is framed by two wheat-stalks, doubtless representing one of the vital crops on which Aksum's prosperity depended. Apart from an early issue (Type 6) of Aphilas, only Gersem (Type 145), one of the last coin-issuing rulers, replaces the profile bust with a frontal one on his gold pieces, though this becomes common – perhaps under Byzantine influence – on silver and bronze coins datable to the sixth century.

Most unusually – and adding extra emphasis to the importance of the royal position in the state – the king's image is again represented on the reverse of the gold coins. But this time he wears not the tiara but a sort of close headcloth or helmet with (usually) three lines at the front, possibly indicating stretch-marks in the cloth or, more probably, an aigrette-like ornament. Endubis alone, founder of the series, was depicted wearing this headcloth style of headgear on both the obverse and the reverse of his gold pieces (Type 1). Possibly the idea of the dual bust, obverse and reverse, derived from the coinage of Arabia Felix on which double busts, royal or divine, also appeared. The Arabian coinage was discontinued, probably in the earlier third century, but doubtless pieces still circulated not too long before the first Aksumite issues. Numbers of silver and bronze coins of several different south Arabian types have been reported from Ethiopia (see Munro-Hay, *Coinage of Arabia Felix*, forthcoming).

On silver and bronze Aksumite coins the headcloth image is the norm for the obverse and reverse until Ouazebas, though other designs are sometimes used on either the obverse or the reverse, such as the facing bust (Type 14, Aphilas) or the wheat-stalk (Types 11 and 13, Aphilas) or the cross (e.g. Type 50). As the series continued, crowned heads appeared on the obverse of these lesser metal pieces too; if the Wazeba Type 16 (AR 2) issue is a genuine one – and the photograph in Vaccaro (1967, no. 16) shows a broken piece which might be genuine – and if it does not in fact belong to Ouazebas (Regoudy 1985) this starts with Wazeba; if not, it commences a little later with the Anonymous (?) Type 66 and with MḤDYS silver (Type 69). On the gold pieces the headcloth bust of the king is often depicted holding a branch-like object, with dots representing perhaps fruits or berries: perhaps a fly-whisk? This item of regalia is later sometimes found on the obverse.

King Aphilas – or perhaps his mint-master – was evidently an innovator. He experimented with fractions and with a number of different designs. His largest gold piece introduced the profile bust wearing the tiara, with a facing bust on a half-weight issue (Type 6). There was also a quarter issue (recently discovered by Bent Juel-Jensen), Type 7, and a tiny one-sixteenth(?) piece (Type 8), with an anepigraphic obverse, the legend occupying the whole field on the reverse. Aphilas also issued two weights of silver, one gilded on the royal bust on the reverse (Type 10), and three different weights of bronze (Types 12–14). This multiplicity of fractions seems to have proved unnecessarily complicated – later kings issuing far fewer types – but the gilded silver became a characteristic of Aksumite coinage.

The phenomenon of gilding might have been instituted to raise the value of the coins of lesser metals: Ousanas was the last king to issue the heavier type of silver, and possibly silver was then scarce in Aksum. Alternatively, it might have been intended to encourage by its opulent appearance the spread of the use of coinage in the remoter reaches of the kingdom, where royal payments for services, or demands for taxes and the like to be paid in coin, could not force its acceptance so easily. Barter would have been the customary method of exchange in most places, except perhaps at the port of Adulis or at other market centres where foreign coinage was already used; an attempt to make the coinage look attractive and valuable might have been behind the original idea of gilding certain pieces. Or, possibly, the gilding was merely a question of prestige, with reference to the sacred nature of the king and the cross. Whatever the case, this difficult and expensive technique, which the Aksumite coinage alone employed, seems to have had some real function, since it persisted almost from beginning to end of the series.

Perhaps the most characteristic reverse motif on silver and bronze coins after Ezana's conversion is the cross (Juel-Jensen 1990ii/1993ii). Ethiopian art has since exploited the cross form to a high degree, but on these coins some of the earliest developments can be seen. The earliest with the cross as a major motif on one face seem to be the silver **BAX ACA** Type 50 with the cross inlaid with gold. Later, Latin and Greek-style crosses, cross-crosslets, diamond-centred crosses inlaid with gold, and other variants were used. It may be – indeed it seems almost certain – that the Aksumite kings, second only after the kings of Armenia to make Christianity the official faith of their state, were the first to put the cross on their coins; it already appears replacing the disc and crescent on gold and bronze coins of the king who first converted to Christianity, Ezana.

The question of the date of the arrival of Christianity in Ethiopia is a vexed one. Some scholars have been very reluctant to accept a fourth-century date for King Ezana and his conversion, endeavouring to divide up the coinage and inscriptions bearing variants of the name Ezana between several kings, depending on whether they show pagan or Christian symbols or phraseology (see particularly Pirenne 1975). Many of these theories seem to me to ignore or misinterpret the very coherent evidence of the coinage and the inscriptions. Even when the existence of a single king Ezana is accepted, the question of the precise date for the conversion remains: whether to accept the Ethiopians' own traditional date of around AD 330 or a later one. In resolving this question, Aksumite numismatics has a primary place.

Study of the style and weight, and, later, measurement of the gold content of the pagan and Christian gold issues bearing the name of Ezanas Bisi Alene (Types 35–7, 47) and Ezana Bisi Alen (Type 49), showed conclusively that the idea that there could have been two or even three kings called Ezana issuing separate series of coins in the fourth, fifth or even sixth centuries was unfounded. The three types fit perfectly according to these criteria into the coinage sequence after the pagan kings at the head of the series, and before all the rest of the Christian kings.

This leaves the question of date. In a recent book (Munro-Hay 1991, p. 202) Ezana's pagan and Christian gold issues with the name written with the euphonic s-ending and weighing up to 2.18g for the pagan coins and up to 2.09g for the Christian type, were paralleled with the standard of the aureus in use in the Roman empire before the currency reform instituted by the Emperor Constantine in 309. Until 324 Constantine's new solidus of 4.54g in the western empire ran parallel to the old heavier aureus of 5.45g still in use in the eastern empire. The theoretical weight of the half-aureus was then 2.72g; that of the new half-solidus about 2.27g. With the defeat of Licinius in 324, the new solidus became universal, spreading to the eastern mints of the empire, the regions with which Aksum had its closest contacts (Sutherland 1967, pp. 93–4; Bruun 1966, pp. 1-4; Kent 1981, pp. 55–7). The first two types of Ezana's gold issue contrasted with another Christian issue of Ezana with the name written without the s-ending and with the weight more or less in conformity with the so-called tremissis of the post-324 Roman reform, at about 1.70g. The Aksumite pieces of this type weigh about 1.53g; subsequent Aksumite gold issues all more or less adhere to this weight.

The earliest Ethiopian gold coins, those of Endubis, seem clearly enough to be associated with the older Roman aureus, the average weight being around the 2.60–2.70g mark, close to the 2.72g weight of the Roman half-solidus. Aphilas, Endubis' successor, used similar weights. But after this the weights drop considerably, the single known gold coin of Wazeba weighing 2.05g, while Ousanas (presumed to be also Ella Amida, Ezana's father) issued gold coins with weights which, in the surviving pieces, vary from 2.56g down to 1.85g.

The problem is, what does this fall of the gold-weight at Aksum signify? The heavier coins of Ousanas could represent half-aurei, the lighter ones post-324 reform half-solidi. This indicates that the change from aureus standard to solidus came in Ousanas' reign, which would thus date from sometime after about 320 (see below) to at least 324/5. Wazeba's single coin does not contribute much, but he seems, from his silver bi-regnal issue with Ousanas, to have been a co-ruler with him at some point, perhaps even around 324/5 as his single coin weighs only 2.05g, seemingly a half-solidus rather than a half-aureus. If Ousanas died in the late 20s of the fourth century, Ezana would then have succeeded under his mother's regency, with the future bishop of Aksum, Frumentius, acting as chief minister for a few more years before his majority and official conversion to Christianity, probably *c.* AD 340. The numismatic evidence thus does not clash with the traditional Ethiopian date for the conversion of about 333 EC (AD 340–41). As noted above, it was previously proposed that the heavier Ezanas gold coins, both pagan and Christian, represented rather light versions of the half-aureus of about 2.72g. However, the fact that none exceeds even the 2.27g of the half-solidus makes it probable that they are intended as half-solidi. Ezana's lighter gold coins would represent the tremissis.

Hahn, in the *Numismatic Chronicle* (1993), suggested that it was in fact Ousanas, Ezana's father, who adopted the new weight standard. He also noted that Aphilas, a predecessor of Ousanas, copied the frontal portrait coins (struck in 320/2) of the Licinii, thus emphasising Aksumite/eastern Roman connections around 320. Aphilas' reign presumably ceased shortly after this. His coins (much commoner, *pace* Hahn, and of a much richer variety than Wazeba's single known gold coin and about twenty-four known examples of his single silver type) closely followed the aureus standard. The weights of his known half-aureus coins range between 2.40 and 2.76g, the quarter-aureus weighs 1.41g, the eighth-aureus 0.66g, and the tiny one-sixteenth-aureus pieces weigh between 0.34 and 0.30g, all fairly accurate fractions of the 5.45g aureus. Incidentally, Hahn is in error in saying that the manifestation of the new creed was limited, on Ezanas' coins, to gold; the bronze coin of Ezanas with a cross, Type 48, omitted in Hahn's 1983 catalogue, indicates that the cross appeared in Ezana's lifetime even on the lesser metals.

The legends on the coins are at first engraved in Greek, on all three metals. Later there is a gradual change, the ancient Ethiopic language, Ge'ez (a Semitic language written with a cursive form of the old southern Arabian alphabet), coming to predominate on the lesser metals. Greek, however, was retained for the gold; an indication of its status in the international trade of the time, when the Greek language had become the lingua franca of the Roman Orient. Wazeba alone of the early coin issuers employed Ge'ez on his gold and silver. On bi-regnal coins (Type 19) of Wazeba and Ousanas, the obverse of Wazeba with its Ge'ez legend contrasts with the Greek on the reverse of Ousana; possibly these two kings reigned together, and one partner decided to issue coins using the local language, the other retaining the Greek. King MḤDYS (his name is only known in unvocalised Ge'ez) appears to have been the first to use Ge'ez on bronze coins, on an issue (Type 70) with a legend apparently inspired by Constantine the Great's famous vision where he saw a cross together with the words 'hoc signo vinces', or by the legend 'hoc signo victor eris' which appeared on Roman coins from the time of Vetranio (350) onwards. In this case, the Ge'ez word *masqal*, cross, is added. A unique MḤDYS gold coin (Type 67; different from the already known forgery Type 68, a cast of his silver Type 69) has been recently discovered, also with the legend in Ge'ez; the piece has been examined (Munro-Hay 1995) to establish its specific gravity, weight, flan type, and size, and completely different though it is from all other Aksumite gold pieces in style, it seems to be genuine. One silver issue of King Ioel, in the sixth century (Type 129), combines the two languages, Ge'ez on the obverse, Greek on the reverse.

At first, the legends merely record the royal name and titles. But later in the fourth century another feature, the use of brief mottoes, becomes customary. The kings of Aksum sent messages to their people by the medium of the coinage legends. Some of the earliest Christian examples – very possibly issued by Ezana himself or an immediate successor – show the cross in the centre surrounded by the words 'May this please the people', doubtless a form of conversion manifesto. Other legends declare 'By the grace of God', or (on MḤDYS coins) 'By this Cross he is victorious'. Later messages read 'Joy and peace to the people', 'Christ is with us', or 'Mercy and peace'.

A number of coins bearing the motto 'Theou Eukharistia' (By the grace of God) date apparently to the fifth century and belong to certain issues emitted by the kings named on the coins as Ousas, Ousanas, Ousana, Nezana and Nezool, as well as Kaleb (Type 97). From study of the al-Madhariba hoard (Munro-Hay 1989ii), the largest collection of Aksumite gold coins ever yet found, die-links connecting coins of Nezana, Nezool and the anonymous gold Type 81 were identified. Also, coins belonging to the kings named Ousas and Ousanas were linked together. In the former case we may have two kings reigning conjointly, or a ruler using two different names; in the second case it seems very probable that Ousas is an abbreviation of Ousana(s). Close resemblances between the Ousas/Ousana(s) series and Kaleb's gold coins would seem to imply that these coins preceded those of Kaleb. Thus, possibly, Ousas/Ousana(s) was identical with Tazena, whom Kaleb (unusually) names as his father on most of his gold issues. Alternatively, this prominent use of his father's name on Kaleb's coinage, and on the single inscription of his so far found, may indicate some sort of dynastic upset, with Kaleb perhaps asserting his legitimacy via these media.

Rare diversions from the standard imagery of the royal busts and crosses are found on two types with an architectural reverse. Three types (117, 125–6), with the reverse legend ZA-YAʿABIYO LA MAD<u>H</u>EN NEGUS (also rendered as LMD<u>H</u>NT-NGS ZYʿBY, Godet 1986) show an arch supported on double columns, sheltering a gold-inlaid cross. A further type (151), of King Arma<u>h</u>, depicts columns and an arch supporting a central gold-inlaid cross flanked by two others, with a key-shaped object under the arch. These pieces may refer – at a guess – to the conquest of Jerusalem by the Persians in AD 614–29, alluding perhaps to Calvary or to the Holy Sepulchre.

A number of anonymous issues were produced, in particular two bronze series, Types 51–2 and Type 76, which were evidently struck in great numbers, probably over a considerable period of time. It is, naturally, difficult to date or attribute these and the several other gold and silver anonymous issues. The first may well belong to an early Christian king of Aksum, possibly one of Ezana's immediate successors, if not to Ezana himself (see below). It is the type which has the widest geographical spread of all Aksumite issues, examples (or copies (?), Type 51) having been found in Meroë, Israel (Jerusalem, Caesarea, Beth-Shean), and Lebanon (supposedly from Baalbek), Turkey (Antioch on the Orontes), as well as in Egypt and at Qana (Bir ʿAli) in Hadhramawt (see, for example, Barkay 1981; Meshorer 1965–6; Milne 1926, 1926ii; Petrie 1889; Waage 1952; Munro-Hay 1991). Two bronze Aksumite coins were found in the river Vaigai at Madurai and at Karur on the Amaravati river in south India (recorded in Mitchiner 1995, p. 81); the latter was of the anonymous type, while the other seems to belong to King M<u>H</u>DYS. More Aksumite bronzes are now reported from Qana in Hadhramawt (pers. comm. Dr A. Sedov). A gold coin of Ousanas bought in Kerala (see Hahn's review already mentioned) may, if it really originated from there, be a further indication of Aksumite-Indian relations in the fourth century; another gold coin of Ousanas also perhaps from India is noted by Juel-Jensen (1994). Similarly, a single Aksumite silver coin, of King Ebana, has been recorded from Shabwa in the Hadhramawt in southern Yemen (Munro-Hay, 1991ii); and, most unusually, a bronze of Wazena was found at Fairlight near Hastings (Juel-Jensen and Munro-Hay 1994).

But gold Aksumite coins from south Arabia are, so far, much better represented than are such coins from Ethiopia itself. They reflect the intimate connections which linked the two sides of the Red Sea in trade, and sometimes politically, from early times. Many, like the coins of the al-Madhariba hoard (Munro-Hay 1989ii), are probably relics of the expedition led by King Kaleb of Aksum around AD 519, which resulted in the conquest of the country and the imposition of a viceroy. Conversely, south Arabian coins, too, are not uncommon from the area of the Aksumite dominion in Ethiopia.

The silver anonymous Type 50, with the cross on the obverse inlaid with gold, may, with the first of the bronze anonymous issues Types 51–2, be datable to a period subsequent to (or at least contemporary with) the issue of Ouazebas' bronze type (Type 54 etc.). This suggestion derives not just from the fact that the appearance of the cross as a reverse type might well be subsequent to the use, customary since Endubis, of two royal images wearing the headcloth on the bronzes (which Ouazebas still retains), but from the results of the analysis of the gold inlays on Aksumite coins undertaken by Russo and Russo (1991). They found that some types of coins – their analysed examples were Aphilas Type 10 and Ouazebas Type 58 – were gilded using thin gold leaf when striking the blanks. These would seem to be the earlier. For all later coins – including the anonymous silver Type 50 – gold-amalgam firing was employed.

The later gold issues, of King Allamidas/'Allamiruis' (Types 115–16), Ella Gabaz (Type 124), Ioel (Types 127–8), Ḥataz/'Iathlia' (Type 136), Israel (Type 143), and Gersem (Types 145–6), are thin-flan pieces, with more or less degenerate Greek legends and badly cut dies. By the sixth century, after King Kaleb's famous expedition of conquest to the Yemen in the late teens of the century – perhaps the origin of his large number of gold issues (Types 91–110) and of some of the gold coins found in the Yemen – Aksum's great days were over. This is reflected in the quality and style of the coinage itself. It is difficult to be specific, but it seems very likely that the coinage continued right to the end of Aksum's life as the capital of the Ethiopian kingdom, probably until about AD 630 (see Munro-Hay 1991). In the upper levels of many of the great structures in the city, or in squatter rooms built around their ruins, coins of the later kings abound. Whatever it was that finished Aksum as a capital – and abroad the Persian conquest of the Yemen around AD 570, their attacks on Roman Egypt and Syria some fifty years later, and the rise of the Arabs in the 630s and 640s were all events which must have helped vitiate the Red Sea trade which had made Aksum wealthy and powerful – the coinage failed to outlast the city itself. It may be that overuse of the land around Aksum and climatic changes left the city's hinterland unable to support a large population any longer, compelling the Ethiopian kings to depart for more fertile districts. With the failure of the Red Sea trading system and the eclipse of their international position, they no longer needed to issue coinage; capital and monetary system were probably abandoned at more or less the same time.

General Bibliography

This bibliography does not include sale catalogues.
The author has not seen those publications marked ★.

ABBADIE, A. D', 1868. 'Observations sur les monnaies éthiopiennes', *Revue Numismatique* XIII (n.s.), pp. 45–62, pl. III.

ALFÖLDI, M. R., 1978. *Antike Numismatik, Teil I, Theorie und Praxis*, Mainz am Rhein, p. 204.

ALTHEIM, F., and STIEHL, R., 1961. 'Die Datierung des Königs Ezana von Aksum', *Klio* 39, pp. 241ff.

ALTHEIM, F., and STIEHL, R., 1968. *Die Araber in der Alten Welt*, vol. IV, p. 508; V/1, pp. 352ff; V/2, pp. 182, 222–3, 267–8, etc.

ANFRAY, F., 1968. 'Les rois d'Aksoum d'après la numismatique', *Journal of Ethiopian Studies* VI, pp. 1–15.

ANZANI, A., 1926. 'Numismatica aksumita', *Rivista Italiana di Numismatica e Scienzi Affini* III, Serie terza, XXXIX, pp. 5–110.

ANZANI, A., 1928. 'Numismatica e storia d'Etiopia, note bibliografiche, nuove osservazioni di numismatica axumita', *Rivista Italiana di Numismatica* V-VI, Serie terza, XLI-XLII, pp. 5–69.

ANZANI, A., 1941. 'Le monete dei re di Aksum, studi supplementari', *Rivista Italiana di Numismatica* I, Serie quarta, XLIII, pp. 49–73, 81–99, 113–29.

ATKINS, F. B., and JUEL-JENSEN, B. E., 1988. 'The gold coinage of Aksum. Further analyses of specific gravity. A contribution to chronology', *Numismatic Chronicle*, pp. 175–80.

ATKINS, F. B., JUEL-JENSEN, B. E., MORTIMER, C., and MUNRO-HAY, S. C., 1991. 'The struck silver coins of the Aksumite king MHDYS and the cast forgery. A reconsideration', *Spink Numismatic Circular* XCIX/2 (March), pp. 39–41.

BARKAY, R., 1981. 'An Axumite coin from Jerusalem', *Israel Numismatic Journal* 5, pp. 57–9.

★BARKAY, R., 1984. 'Coinage of the Kingdom of Aksum' (in Hebrew), *Qadmoniot* 17/2–3, pp. 86–8.

BARRANDON, J.-N., GODET, E., and MORRISON, C., 1990. 'Le monnayage d'or axoumite: une altération particulière', *Revue Numismatique* XXXII, pp. 186–211.

BENDALL, S., 1986–7. 'A note on "An Axumite coin from Jerusalem" ', *Israel Numismatic Journal* 9, p. 91, pl. 32, 3–4.

BOURLIER, P., 1968. 'Numismatique axoumite', *Collectionneurs et Collections numismatiques*, Paris, pp. 67–70.

BROWNE, G. E., 1992. 'Some remarks on Axumite coin legends', *Orbis Aethiopicus* II, pp. 292–6.

BRUNTON, G., 1927. *Qau and Badari*, vol. III, London, p. 30.

BRUUN, P. M., 1966. *The Roman Imperial Coinage*, vol. VII, London.

BUTTREY, T.V., 1971–2. 'Axumite addenda', *Rassegna di Studi Etiopici* 25, pp. 44–52.

CARRADICE, I., 1989. 'Coinage of a forgotten kingdom', *British Museum Society Bulletin* 62, pp. 28–9.

CASSON, L., 1989. *Periplus Maris Erythraei*, Princeton.

CLARK, W. L., 1948. 'Coins from Axum', *ANS Museum Notes* III, pp. 125–9, pl. XXII.

CONTENSON, H. DE, 1959. 'Les fouilles à Axoum en 1957. Rapport préliminaire', *Annales d'Ethiopie* III, p. 32.

CONTENSON, H. DE, 1963. 'Les fouilles à Axoum en 1958. Rapport préliminaire', *Annales d'Ethiopie* V, p. 4ff.

CONTENSON, H. DE, 1976. 'A propos d'une révision de la chronologie axoumite', *L'Anthropologie* 80, pp. 520–21.

CONTI ROSSINI, C., 1927. 'Monete Aksumite', *Africa Italiana* I, pp. 179–212.

CONTI ROSSINI, C., 1928. 'Recensione di "Numismatica Axumita" di Arturo Anzani', *Oriente Moderno* 3, pp. 137–41.

CONTI ROSSINI, C., 1935. 'Numismatica Etiopica', *Rassegna Numismatica* 5 and 6 (anno XXXII), pp. 179–81.

CÔTE, C. Unpublished corrrespondence with Anzani *et al.* relating to Aksumite coinage, preserved in the Bibliothèque Nationale, Paris.

DEWING, H. B. (ed. and trans.), 1914. *Procopius, History of the Wars.* Loeb, London.

DILLMANN, A., 1879. 'Über die Anfänge des Axumitischen Reiches', *Abhandlung der Königlichen Akademie der Wissenschaften zu Berlin aus dem Jahre 1878*, Berlin, pp. 226–30.

DORESSE, J., 1957. 'Sur une monnaie axoumite. . .', in *L'Empire du Prêtre-Jean*, vol. I, Paris, pp. 278–82.

DRESSEL, H., 1898. 'Erwerbungen des Königlichen Münzcabinets in den Jahren 1890–1897', *Zeitschrift für Numismatik* XXV, pp. 238–9.

DROUIN, E., 1882. 'Les listes royales éthiopiennes et leur autorité historique', *Revue Archéologique* XLIV, pp 99–115, 153–72, 206–17 (appendix, king lists, pp. 218–24), pl. XX.

★DROUIN, E., 1882. 'Observations sur les monnaies éthiopiennes', *Revue Archéologique*, p. 19.

EGLSEER, W. R., 1976. 'Axum', *Kricheldorfs Berichte* 95, pp. 185–90.

FITZWILLIAM MUSEUM, CAMBRIDGE, 1982. *The Annual Reports of the Syndicate and of the Friends of the Fitzwilliam for the Year ending 31 December 1982*, p. 29.

FREEMAN-GRENVILLE, G. S. P., 1992–3. 'Jerusalem, Aksum and Aachen', *Israel Numismatic Journal* 12, pp. 80–86, pls 10–20.

FRIEDBERG, R., 1965. *Gold Coins of the World*, New York, pp. 89–90.

FRIEDLÄNDER, J., 1879. 'Die Erwerbungen des Königliche Münzkabinets vom 1 April 1878 bis 1 April 1879', *Zeitschrift für Numismatik* VII, p. 229, Taf. IV/4.

GILL, D., 1991. *The Coinage of Ethiopia, Eritrea and Italian Somalia*, Garden City, New York.

GÖBL, R., 1978. *Antike Numismatik*, Munich, pp. 115–16, 220–21. (See also note in *Hamburger Beitrage zur Numismatik* 17, pp. 735–6.)

GODET, E., 1986. 'Bilan de recherches récentes en numismatique axoumite', *Revue Numismatique* XXVIII, pp. 174–209.

★GODET, E., 1991. 'Ethiopie antique et moderne', in *A Survey of Numismatic Research*, Brussels.

GORNUNG, M., 1973. 'Aksumskie Monetoi', *Soobshcheniya Gosudarstvennogo Ermitazha* (Reports of the Hermitage Museum) XXXVII, pp. 64–8.

HAHN, W. R. O., 1983. 'Die Münzprägung des Axumitischen Reiches', *Litterae Numismaticae Vindobonenses* 2, pp. 113–80, Taf. 12–15.

HAHN, W. R. O., 1984. 'The numismatic evidence for the reconstruction of the Aksumite royal line', *ANS Museum Notes* 29, pp. 159–79.

HAHN, W. R. O., 1984ii. 'Further reconsiderations on the chronology of the coinage of Aksum', *Jahrbuch für Numismatik und Geldgeschichte* XXXIV, pp. 127–34.

HAHN, W. R. O., 1987. 'Die Vokalisierung Axumitischer Münzaufschriften als Datierungselement', *Litterae Numismaticae Vindobonenses* 3, pp. 217–24.

★HAHN, W. R. O., 1988. 'Aksumite coins in Southern Arabia and in Palestine', *Proceedings of the 9th Conference of Ethiopian Studies, Moscow, 26–29 August 1986.*

HAHN, W. R. O., 1988ii. 'Some remarks on the metal composition of Aksumite silver coins', *Metallurgy in Numismatics* 2, pp. 17–21.

HAHN, W. R. O., 1989. 'A numismatic contribution to the dating of the Aksumite king Sembrouthes', *Proceedings of the 8th International Conference of Ethiopian Studies 1984*, vol. 2, pp. 11–13.

HAHN, W. R. O., 1993. Review of S. C. Munro-Hay, *Aksum* (1991), *Numismatic Chronicle*, pp. 316–19.

HALÉVY, J., 1873. 'Monnaies d'Abyssinie', *Comptes rendus de la Société française de numismatique et d'archéologie*, pp. 224–6.

HALÉVY, J., 1874. *Mélanges d'épigraphie et d'archéologie sémitique*, Paris, pp. 126–46. Halévy also makes brief reference to Aksumite coins in 'L'inscription éthiopienne de l'obélisque près de Matara', *Revue Sémitique d'Epigraphie et d'Histoire ancienne* IV (1896), pp. 363–5.

★HEUGLIN, T. VON, 1863. 'Beschreibung einiger Äthiopischen Kupfermünzen, Adoa 1861', *Zeitschrift der Deutschen Morgenländischen Gesellschaft*, p. 377; see also *Reise nach Abissinien. . .*, Jena 1868, p. 153.

HILL, G. F., 1917. 'Greek coins acquired by the British Museum, 1914–1916', *Numismatic Chronicle*, pp. 27–30.

HILL, G. F., 1922. 'Greek coins acquired by the British Museum', *Numismatic Chronicle*, pp. 174–5, pl. VII; also 1926, pp. 134–6, pl. VI/24.

HILL, G. F., 1922ii. *Catalogue of the Greek Coins of Arabia, Mesopotamia and Persia*, BMC 28, London 1922, p. liii.

HUNTINGFORD, G. W. B., 1980. *The Periplus of the Erythraean Sea*, Hakluyt Society, London.

JUEL-JENSEN, B. E., 1985. 'An apparently undescribed Aksumite gold coin from the reign of King Ezana', *Spink Numismatic Circular* XCIII/3 (April), p. 85.

JUEL-JENSEN, B. E., 1986. 'Ousanas I – Ezanas – Ousanas II. Further evidence for the chronological sequence of some early Aksumite coins', *Spink Numismatic Circular* XCIV/8 (October), pp. 255–8.

JUEL-JENSEN, B. E., 1987. 'A new silver coin of King Wazena of Aksum', *Spink Numismatic Circular* XCV/7 (September), pp. 219–20.

JUEL-JENSEN, B. E., 1987ii. 'Vaccaro's Aksumite "King Alelan": a ghost laid', *Spink Numismatic Circular* XCV/8 (October), p. 255.

JUEL-JENSEN, B. E., 1988. 'Three undescribed gold coins of King Kaleb of Aksum', *Spink Numismatic Circular* XCVI/9 (November), pp. 279–81.

JUEL-JENSEN, B. E., 1989. 'Was the design of one of Offa's coins inspired by the silver of King Ebana of Aksum?', *Spink Numismatic Circular* XCVII/9 (November), p. 296.

JUEL-JENSEN, B. E., 1990. 'A modern forgery of a gold coin of the Aksumite king Ousanas I', *Spink Numismatic Circular* XCVIII/10 (December), p. 349.

JUEL-JENSEN, B. E., 1990ii. 'The evolution of the Ethiopian cross', paper read to the Second International Conference of Ethiopian Art, Nieborow, Poland, September 1990, published privately, Oxford, and in *Aspects of Ethiopian Art from Ancient Axum to the Twentieth Century*, London 1993, pp. 17–27 (=1993ii).

JUEL-JENSEN, B. E., 1991. 'A new Aksumite coin from the Early Christian Period', *Spink Numismatic Circular* XCIX/2 (March), p. 39.

JUEL-JENSEN, B. E., 1993. 'An anonymous new Aksumite silver coin from the Early Christian Period', *Spink Numismatic Circular* CI/1 (February), pp. 3–4.

JUEL-JENSEN, B. E., 1993ii. See 1990ii above.

JUEL-JENSEN, B. E., 1994. 'A gold coin of Ousanas of Aksum struck from hitherto unpublished dies', *Spink Numismatic Circular* CII/5 (June), p. 112.

JUEL-JENSEN, B. E., and ATKINS, B., 1994. 'A new quarter aureus completes the series of gold coins of King Aphilas of Aksum', *Spink Numismatic Circular* CII/3 (April), pp. 104–5.

JUEL-JENSEN, B. E., and MUNRO-HAY, S. C., 1994. 'Further examples of coins of Offa inspired by Aksumite designs', *Spink Numismatic Circular* CII/6 (July), pp. 256–7.

KAMMERER, A., 1926. 'Les monnaies d'Aksum du Cabinet des Médailles', in *Essai sur l'histoire antique d'Abyssinie*, Paris, annexe IV, pp. 154–70.

KAMMERER, A., 1926ii. 'Les monnaies abyssins de la collection Muncharjee d'Aden', *Revue Numismatique* 28, pp. 41–51.

KAMMERER, A., 1929. 'Ce que révèle la numismatique', in *La Mer Rouge, l'Abyssinie et l'Arabie depuis l'antiquité*, vol. I/iii, Cairo, ch. 6, pp. 220ff.

KAMMERER, A., 1934. 'Numismatique d'Aksum (Abyssinie antique). Nouvelle monnaie du roi Esbael (fin du Ve ou début du VIe siècle de notre ère)', *Revue Numismatique*, 4e série, vol. 37, pp. 37–43.

KENNER, F., 1862. 'Über das Münzrecht und die Goldpräge der Könige der Axumiten', *Sitzungsberichte der Philosophisch-Historischen Classe der Kaiserlichen Akademie der Wissenschaften* 39, pp. 554–6.

KENT, J. P. C., 1981. *The Roman Imperial Coinage*, vol. VIII, London.

*KINDLER, A., 1988. 'Relations between Israel and Ethiopia in late Roman and Byzantine times according to numismatic discoveries' (in Hebrew), in Matouk, T., *Jews and Samaritans in Byzantine Israel*, Jerusalem, pp. 106–11.

LANGLOIS, V., 1859. 'Royaume des Axumites', appendix in *Numismatique des Arabes avant l'Islamisme*, Paris, pp. 148–58, pl. IV.

LITTMANN, E., 1913. *Deutsche Aksum-Expedition. Reisebericht der Expedition, Topographie und Geschichte Aksums*. I, iii, *Zur Geschichte Aksums*, Berlin, pp. 46–60, Taf. III.

LITTMANN, E., 1925. 'Eine neue Goldmünze des Königs Israel von Aksum', *Zeitschrift für Numismatik* XXXV, pp. 272–4, Taf. XIV/8.

LONGPÉRIER, A. DE, 1868. 'Monnaies des rois d'Ethiopie (Nagast d'Aksum en Ethiopie)', *Revue Numismatique* XIII (n.s.), p. 28, pl. II.

LOWICK, N. M., 1969. 'Aksumite coins', *British Museum Quarterly* XXXIV/3–4, pp. 148–51, pls XL-XLII.

MESHORER, Y., 1965–6. 'An Axumite coin from Caesarea', *Israel Numismatic Journal* III, 1965–6, p. 76, pl. XV.2.

MILNE, J. G., 1926. 'The currency of Egypt in the fifth century', *Numismatic Chronicle*, p. 92.

MILNE, J. G., 1926ii. 'Feudal currency in Roman Egypt', *Ancient Egypt*, p. 5.

MITCHINER, M., 1978. *Oriental Coins and their Values*, vol. I, pp. 96–100.

MITCHINER, M., 1995. *Coin Circulation in Southernmost India, circa 200 BC to AD 1835*, Indian Institute of Research in Numismatic Studies, Nasik, India.

MORDINI, A., 1945. 'Informazioni preliminari sui risultati delle mie ricerche in Etiopia dal 1939–1944', *Rassegna di Studi Etiopici* IV, p. 150.

MORDINI, A., 1949. 'Su di un nuovo titolo regale aksumita', *Rassegna di Studi Etiopici* VIII, pp. 7–11.

MORDINI, A., 1959. 'Appunti di numismatica Aksumita', *Annales d'Ethiopie* III, pp. 179–83.

MORDINI, A., 1960. 'Gli aurei kushana del convento di Dabra-Dammo', *Atti del Convegno internazionale di studi Etiopici (Roma 1959)*, Rome, Accademia Nazionale dei Lincei, pp. 249–54.

MORDINI, A., 1967. 'Gold Kushana coins in the convent of Dabra Dammo'. *Journal of the Numismatic Society of India* XXIX, pp. 19–25.

MUNRO-HAY, S. C., 1978. 'The chronology of Aksum: a reappraisal of the history and development of the Aksumite state from numismatic and archaeological evidence', unpublished Ph.D. thesis, School of Oriental and African Studies, London 1978, pp. 1–274.

MUNRO-HAY, S. C., 1979. 'MHDYS and Ebana, kings of Aksum: some problems of dating and identity', *Azania* XIV, pp. 21–30.

MUNRO-HAY, S. C., 1979ii. 'Ezana and Ezanas: inscriptions and coins', *Abbay* 10, pp. 87ff.

MUNRO-HAY, S. C., 1980. 'Ezana (Ezana and Ezanas): some numismatic comments', *Azania* XV, pp. 109–19.

MUNRO-HAY, S. C., 1980–81. 'Aksumite addenda: the existence of "Bisi Anioskal" ', *Rassegna di Studi Etiopici* XXVIII, pp. 57–60.

MUNRO-HAY, S. C., 1981–2. 'A tyranny of sources: the history of Aksum from its coinage', *Northeast African Studies* 3/3, pp. 1–16.

MUNRO-HAY, S. C., 1982. 'A new issue of King Nezool of Aksum in the collection of the American Numismatic Society', *ANS Museum Notes* 27, pp. 181–4.

MUNRO-HAY, S. C., 1984. *The Coinage of Aksum*, New Delhi and Butleigh.

MUNRO-HAY, S. C., 1984ii. 'Aksumite chronology: some reconsiderations', *Jahrbuch für Numismatik und Geldgeschichte* XXXIV, pp. 107–26. Also published in *Proceedings of the 8th International Conference of Ethiopian Studies 1984*, vol. 2, Addis Ababa 1989, pp. 27–40.

MUNRO-HAY, S. C., 1984iii. 'The Geez and Greek palaeography of the coinage of Aksum', *Azania* XIX, pp. 134–44.

MUNRO-HAY, S. C., 1984iv. 'An African monetarised economy in ancient times', *Proceedings of the Second International Conference on Indian Ocean Studies, Perth, 1984*, Perth, Western Australia, section E (Maritime studies: shipping, trade and port-cities), no pagination.

MUNRO-HAY, S. C., 1986. *The Munro-Hay Collection of Aksumite Coins*, Supplemento no. 48 of the Annali, Istituto Universitario Orientale, Naples, pp. 1–89, pls 1–39.

MUNRO-HAY, S. C., 1987. 'Aksumite silver coinage: some variant types in the Brereton Collection', *Numismatic Chronicle* 147, pp. 174–5.

MUNRO-HAY, S. C., 1988 'The dating of Ezana(s) and Frumentius', *Rassegna di Studi Etiopici* XXXIII, pp. 111–27.

MUNRO-HAY, S. C., 1989. *Excavations at Aksum: an account of research at the ancient Ethiopian capital directed in 1972–4 by the late Dr. Neville Chittick*, Memoirs of the British Institute in Eastern Africa, no. 10, London.

MUNRO-HAY, S. C., 1989ii. 'The al-Madhariba hoard of gold Aksumite and Late Roman coins', *Numismatic Chronicle* 149, pp. 83–100, pls 22–9.

MUNRO-HAY, S. C., 1990. 'A new silver coin of King Aphilas of Aksum', *Numismatic Chronicle*, p. 238.

MUNRO-HAY, S. C., 1991. *Aksum. An African Civilisation of Late Antiquity*, Edinburgh University Press.

MUNRO-HAY, S. C., 1991ii. 'The coinage of Shabwa (Hadhramawt) and other ancient South Arabian coinage in the National Museum, Aden', *Syria* LXVIII, pp. 393–418; also in the report of the Institut français d'archéologie du Proche-Orient, publication hors-série no. 19, *Fouilles de Shabwa* II, 1991.

MUNRO-HAY, S. C., 1991iii. 'Un trésor de pièces romaines et éthiopiennes découvert près d'Aden', *Archéologia* 271 (September), pp. 50–51.

MUNRO-HAY, S. C., 1991–2. 'Forgeries of the Aksumite series', *American Journal of Numismatics*, second series 3–4, pp. 49–64.

MUNRO-HAY, S. C., 1993. 'Aksumite coinage', in *African Zion, the Sacred Art of Ethiopia*, catalogue by M. Heldman with S. C. Munro-Hay, New Haven and London, pp. 101–16.

MUNRO-HAY, S. C., 1994. 'The iconography of Aksumite coinage', paper read to the Second International Conference of Ethiopian Art, Nieborow, Poland, October 1990, and published in Henze, P. (ed.), *Aspects of Ethiopian Art from Ancient Axum to the Twentieth Century*, London, pp. 28–32.

MUNRO-HAY, S. C., 1995. 'A new gold coin of King MHDYS of Aksum', *Numismatic Chronicle* 155, pp. 275–7.

MUNRO-HAY, S. C., forthcoming. *Coinage of Arabia Felix* (Staatliches Museum für Völkerkunde, Munich).

MUNRO-HAY, S. C., and JUEL-JENSEN, B., 1995. *Aksumite Coinage*, London.

MUNRO-HAY, S. C., ODDY, A., and COWELL, M., 1988. 'The gold coinage of Aksum: new analyses and their significance for chronology', *Metallurgy and Numismatics* 2, pp. 1–16.

ODDY, A., and MUNRO-HAY, S. C., 1980. 'The specific gravity analysis of the gold coins of Aksum', *Metallurgy and Numismatics* 1, pp. 73–82, pls 2–4.

PANKHURST, R. K. P., 1975. 'The Greek coins of Aksum', *Abba Salama* 6, pp. 70–83.

PANKHURST, R. K. P., 1979. 'Ethiopia and Sudan: Aksumite currency', in *A Survey of Numismatic Research, 1972–1977*, no. 5, Berne, pp. 413–15.

PARIBENI, R., 1907 (1908). 'Ricerche nel luogo dell'antica Adulis (Colonia Eritrea)', *Monumenti antichi, Reale Accademia dei Lincei* XVIII, col. 437–572. Also Rome, Tip. Lincei, 1908.

PETRIE, W. M. F., 1889. *Hawara, Biahmu and Arsinoë*, London, p. 13, pl. XXIV.

PIRENNE, J., 1975. 'Le cadre chronologique de l'histoire éthiopienne du IVe au VIe siècle', *Actes du XXIXe Congrès Internationale des Orientalistes: Etudes Sémitiques*, Paris, pp. 48–54.

PIRENNE, J., 1975ii. 'L'imbroglio de trois siècles de chronologie aksumite, IVe-VIe s.', *Documents pour servir à l'histoire des civilisations éthiopiennes* 6, pp. 49–58.

PIRENNE, J., 1985. Review of S. Munro-Hay, 'Coinage of Aksum', in *Revue Numismatique* XXVII, pp. 242–6.

PIVA, A., 1907. 'Una civiltà scomparsa dell'Eritrea, e gli scavi archeologici nella regione di Cheren', *Nuova Antologia* (March), pp. 325–35.

PRIDEAUX, W. F., 1881. 'On the coins of Charibael, king of the Homerites and Sabaeans', *Journal of the Asiatic Society of Bengal* I, p. 99, pl. X/8.

PRIDEAUX, W. F., 1884. 'The coins of the Axumite dynasty', *Numismatic Chronicle*, 3rd series, IV, pp. 205–19, plus 'Postscript' in *NC*, 3rd series, V, 1885, p. 66.

PUGLISI, S., 1941. 'Primi risultati delle indagini compiute dalle missione Archeologica di Aksum', *Africa Italiana* VIII/3–4, anno XIX, pp. 95–153, cf. p. 114ff.

REGOUDY, F., 1985. 'Chronologie des rois d'Axoum. Approche numismatique', unpublished thesis, Centre de recherches africaines, University of Paris-I, Panthéon-Sorbonne, Paris.

RÜPPELL, E., 1838–40. *Reise in Abessinien*, Frankfurt am Main, vol. I, pp. XVff; vol. II, pp. 334, 429, atlas Taf. VIII, 3, 6, and 7.

RÜPPELL, E., 1845–6. 'On an unedited coin of one of the early kings of Abyssinia', *Numismatic Chronicle* 8, pp. 121–2.

RUSSO, F., 1991. 'Sulla monetazione di Aksum', *Memorie dell'Accademia Italiana di Studi Filatelici e Numismatici* 4, 3, pp. 85–97.

RUSSO, F., and RUSSO, G., 1991. 'Sugli intarsi in oro nella monetazione aksumite', *Bollettino di Numismatica* 3, pp. 144–60.

SALLET, A. VON, 1884. Summary of Drouin 1882 (see above), in 'Literatur', *Zeitschrift für Numismatik* XI, pp. 176–7.

SALLET, A. VON, 1887. 'Der Erwerbungen des Königlichen Münzcabinets vom 1 April 1886 bis 1 April 1887', *Zeitschrift für Numismatik* XV, pp. 15–17, Taf. I/12.

SALLET, A. VON, 1892. 'Die Erwerbungen des Königlichen Münzkabinets vom 1 April 1889 bis 1 April 1890', *Zeitschrift für Numismatik* XVIII, pp. 201–2.

SAUTER, R., 1979. 'Monnaie d'argent inédite du roi MHDYS', *Azania* XIV, pp. 27–8 (appendix to Munro-Hay 1979 above).

SCHLUMBERGER, G., 1886. 'Monnaies inédites des Ethiopiens et des Himyarites', *Revue Numismatique*, pp. 356–71.

SCHLUMBERGER, G., 1887. 'Une nouvelle monnaie royale Ethiopienne, monnaie d'or du négus Kaleb, roi d'Aksum, conquérant de l'Yémen au VIe siècle', Académie des Inscriptions et Belles-lettres, *Comptes rendus des séances de l'année 1886*, 4e série, XIV, no. VII, p. 231.

SCHNEIDER, R., 1974. 'Trois nouvelles inscriptions royales d'Axoum', *IV Congresso Internazionale di Studi Etiopici, Accad. dei Lincei, Rome 1972*, pp. 767–86.

SCHNEIDER, R., 1976. 'A propos de l'imbroglio de trois siècles de chronologie aksumite, IVe à Ve s.', *Documents pour servir à l'histoire des civilisations éthiopiennes* 7, pp. 41ff.

SCHOLZ, P., 1984. 'Auf den Spuren der äthiopischen Vergangenheit zwischen dem Niltal und Arabia Felix', *Antike Welt. Zeitschrift für Archäologie und Kulturgeschichte*, 15. Jahrgang, Heft 3, pp. 1–34 (cf. Abb. 41).

SHAHID, I., 1971. *The Martyrs of Najran*, Subsidia Hagiographica 49, Brussels.

SUNDSTRÖM, R., 1907. 'Letter to Dr. Enno Littmann', in Littmann, E., 'Preliminary report of the Princeton University Expedition to Abyssinia', *Zeitschrift für Assyriologie und verwandte Gebiete* XX, pp. 172ff, cf. pp. 180–81.

SUTHERLAND, C. H.V., 1967. *The Roman Imperial Coinage*, vol. VI, London.

SZYMUSIAK, J. M., 1958. *Athanasius, Apologia ad Constantium Imperatorem*, Paris.

TEDESCO-ZAMMARANO, V., 1947. 'Contributo alla numismatica Aksumita', *Numismatica* XIII, pp. 8–10.

★TOURAIEFF, B. A., 1901. 'Dvi Aksumskiya Monetvi imperatorskog v Ermitaja' (Two Aksumite coins in the Imperial Hermitage Museum), *Notes of the Classical Division of the Imperial Russian Archaeological Society* I, pp. 44–9.

TRINGALI, G., 1973. 'Due aurei Aksumiti inediti esposti all'Asmara Expo 72', *Journal of Ethiopian Studies* XI/1, pp. 209–11.

TRINGALI, G., 1980. 'Numismatica Aksumita: un argento di Afilas', *Quaderni di Studi Etiopici* 1, pp. 58–9.

VACCARO, F., 1964. 'Numismatica Aksumita', *Bollettino dell'Eritrea* 3, pp. 63–5.

VACCARO, F., 1967. *Le Monete di Aksum*, Mantua.

WAAGE, D., 1952. *Antioch-on-the-Orontes*, vol. IV/ii, *Greek, Roman, Byzantine and Crusaders' Coins*, Princeton, London and The Hague, p. 171.

WALBURG, R., 1980. 'Sechs unpublizierte axumitische Goldmünzen aus Privatbesitz', *Boreas* 3, pp. 174–80, Taf. 22.

WALBURG, R., 1983. 'Die Sammlung Altheim-Stiehl', *Paideuma* 29, pp. 223–86.

WEST, V., 1986. 'An Aksumite concordance', *Spink Numismatic Circular* XCIV/6 (July), pp. 184–5.

WEST V., 1987. 'A variety of King Ouazebas of Aksum', *Spink Numismatic Circular* XCV/2 (March), p. 39.

WOOD, H., 1937. *The Coinage of Ethiopia*, New York (11pp.).

WRIGHT, W., 1868. 'Aus Briefen des Hrn. W. Wright in London an Prof. Rödiges', *Zeitschrift der Deutschen Morgenländischen Gesellschaft* XXII, p. 554.

Chronology

Catalogue

The Pagan Period, *c.* AD 270–340

Endubis
Gold
Type 1 (Endubis AV 1; Munro-Hay 1984, p. 45)

Obv. Head and shoulders bust r., wearing headcloth with rays at forehead and triangular ribbon behind, framed by two wheat-stalks. Disc and crescent at top. Greek legend ENDYBICᴗBACIΛEYC (King Endubis).

Rev. As obv. but legend AξWMITWᴗBICIΔAXY (Of the Aksumites man of Dakhu). (N.B. Aksumite coins always use ξ for Ξ and W for Ω; in addition all coins of Endubis and Aphilas employ a special form of A, consisting of Λ with a dot underneath.)

1	1969–6–24–1	2.81	12:00
2	1989–5–18–1	2.64	12:00
3	1989–5–18–2	2.38	12:00

Endubis
Silver
Type 2 (Endubis AR 1; Munro-Hay 1984, p. 46)

Obv. and rev. as above, without the wheat-stalks. A variant has the letter I of BACIΛEYC missing.

4	1968–4–1–1	2.17	12:00
5	1976–10–16–1	2.31	12:00
6	1989–5–18–3	2.22	12:00
7	1989–5–18–4	2.36	12:00
8	1989–5–18–5	2.26	12:00
9	1989–5–18–6	1.94	12:00

Endubis
Bronze
Type 3 (Endubis AE 1; Munro-Hay 1984, p. 47)

Obv. and rev. as above.

Aphilas
Gold
Types 4–5 (Aphilas AV 2–2a; Munro-Hay 1984, p. 49; J-J 191)

Obv. Half-length bust r., draped and crowned, holding spear or stick, between wheat-stalks. Disc and crescent at top. Greek legend AΦIΛACᴗBACIΛEYC (King Aphilas), or (Type 4i) sometimes divided to read AΦ IΛACᴗBACIΛEYC.
Type 5 differs in that the spear the king holds divides the obverse legend: AΦIΛACᴗBACIΛE YC.

Rev. As obv., but wearing headcloth, holding a branch with berries (?), possibly representing a fly-whisk: AξWMITWNᴗBICIΔIMHΛH (Of the Aksumites man of Dimele).

On both sides there may be occasional reversed or badly written letters.

Aphilas
Gold
Type 6 (Aphilas AV 3; Munro-Hay 1984, p. 50; J-J 79)

Obv. Facing bust, crowned, holding sword l. Disc and crescent at top. Greek legend: AΦIΛΛᴗBACIΛI (Ki[ng] Aphila[s]).

Rev. Half-length bust r., wearing headcloth, holding branch with berries. Disc and crescent at top. Greek legend, abbreviated: Aξ[monogram WMA?]ᴗBICIΔIH ([of the] Aks[umites] man of Di[mel]e).

Aphilas
Gold
Type 7 (Juel-Jensen and Atkins 1994; J-J 404)

Obv. Half-length bust r., wearing headcloth, holding branch with berries (?). Disc and crescent at top. Greek legend: AΦIΛᴗACB (Aphilas K. . .).

Rev. Half-length bust r., wearing headcloth, holding branch with berries (?). Disc and crescent at top. Greek legend continued from obv.: ACIΛᴗEYC (. . .ing).

Aphilas
Gold
Type 8 (Aphilas AV 1; Munro-Hay 1984, p. 48)

Obv. Head and shoulders bust r., wearing headcloth. Disc and crescent r. (missing on Anzani 4, in the Hermitage Museum, St Petersburg).
Rev. Four-line Greek legend: ΑΦΙ ΛΑC ΒΑCΙ ΛΕΥ (Kin[g] Aphilas).

10	1961–10–3–1	0.31	12:00
11	1989–5–18–7	0.33	12:00

Aphilas
Silver
Type 9 (Aphilas AR 1; Munro-Hay 1984, p. 51; J-J 192)

Obv. Head and shoulders bust r., wearing headcloth. Disc and crescent at top. Greek legend all round: ΑΦΙΛΑCᴗΒΑCΙΛΕ ΥC (King Aphilas).
Rev. As obv.: ΑξWΜΙΤWΝᴗΒΙCΙΔΙΜΗΛΗ (Of the Aksumites man of Dimele).

There may be occasional variant letter forms or reversals.

Aphilas
Silver
Type 10 (Aphilas AR 2; Munro-Hay 1984, p. 52)

Obv. Head and shoulders bust r., wearing headcloth. Disc and crescent at top. Greek legend: ΑΦΙΛΑᴗΒΑCΙΛΙ (Ki[ng] Aphila).
Rev. Small head and shoulders bust r., wearing headcloth, in circle. Area inside circle gilded. Disc and crescent at top. Greek legend all round: ΙΑΦΙΛΑCΒᴗΑCΙΛΕΥC (King Iaphilas).

There may be occasional variant letter forms.

12	1969–6–24–2	0.88	12:00
13	1989–5–18–8	1.03	12:00
14	1989–5–18–9	0.84	12:00
15	1989–5–18–10	0.73	10:00
16	1989–5–18–11	0.62	12:00
17	1989–5–18–12	0.79	12:00
18	1989–5–18–13	0.82	12:00
19	1989–5–18–14	0.95	12:00

Aphilas
Silver
Type 11 (Aphilas AR 3; Munro-Hay 1990, p. 238)

Obv. As Type 9 above.
Rev. Wheat-stalk centre field, breaking the legend at the top. Greek legend: [monogram AM?]WξΑ ΗΙΔΙCΙΒ (retrograde) (Of the Aksu[mites] man of Dim[ele]).

Aphilas
Bronze
Type 12 (Aphilas AE 1; Munro-Hay 1984, p. 53)

Obv. Head and shoulders bust facing, wearing headcloth (?). Disc and crescent at top (?). Greek legend: ΑΦΙΛΑCᴗΒΑCΙΛΕΥ C (King Aphilas).
Rev. Small head and shoulders bust r., wearing headcloth, in circle closed by dot at top and bottom. Disc and crescent above. Greek legend all round: ΑξWΜΙΤWΝᴗΒΙCΙΔΙΜΗΛΗ (Of the Aksumites man of Dimele).

20	1873–0–0	4.84	11:00

Aphilas
Bronze
Type 13 (Aphilas AE 2; Munro-Hay 1984, p. 54; J-J 193, 396)

Obv. Head and shoulders bust r., wearing headcloth. Disc and crescent at top. Greek legend: ΑΦΙΛΑCΒΑᴗCΙΛΕΥCΑξW (King Aphilas of the Aksu. . .); some read . . .CΙΛΥΕC..
Rev. Wheat-stalk centre field. Greek legend all round: ΜΙΤWΝΒΙ CΙ ΔΙΜΗΛΗ (. . .mites, man of Dimele). A variant (Juel-Jensen coll., J-J 396) shows the legend written as . . .ΙΜΙΛΗ, and there are other variants as well, e.g. CΙΔΜΙΛΗ (Munro-Hay 1986, 17–18, J-J 193).

Aphilas
Bronze
Type 14 (Aphilas AE 3; Munro-Hay 1984, p. 55; J-J 194)

Obv. Head and shoulders bust facing, wearing headcloth. Disc and crescent at top. Greek legend: ΑΦΙΛΑCᴗΒΑCΙΛΕΥ C (King Aphilas).
Rev. Head and shoulders bust r., wearing headcloth. Disc and crescent at top. Greek legend all round: Α(ξ)WΜΙΤWΝᴗᴗΒΙCΙΔΙΜΗΛΗ (Of the A[ks]umites, man of Dimele). The second letter of the legend is not clear on any example.

Wᴢʙ (Wazeba)
Gold
Type 15 (Wazeba AV 1; Munro-Hay 1984, p. 67; BN N.3 458)

Obv. Half-length bust to r., crowned, holding spear, between two wheat-stalks. Ge'ez monogram WZB above head. (Disc and ?) crescent at top. Ge'ez legend: ወዘበነገሠአክሱᴗመበአበየዘ ገለየ (WZB King of Aksum man of ZGLY). WZB is conventionally vocalised as Wazeb or Wazeba.
Rev. Half-length bust r., wearing headcloth, holding

curved sceptre (?). Dotted circle and two curved lines surround head, enclosed by two wheat-stalks. Ge'ez monogram WZB above head. Crescent and two dots at top. Ge'ez legend: **ወዘበነገሠአከሰመ◡በአሰየዘገለየ** (Wazeba King of Aksum man of ZGLY).

WZB (Wazeba)
Silver
Type 16 (Wazeba AR 2; Munro-Hay 1984, p. 69)

Obv. Half-length bust to r., crowned, holding wheat-stalk, between two Ge'ez monograms WZB. Ge'ez legend: **ወዘበ ነገሠ** (King Wazeba).

Rev. Half-length bust to r., crowned, holding spear, flanked by two Ge'ez monograms WZB.

No legend.

No certainly genuine example of this type has yet been noted.

Wazeba
Silver
Types 17–18 (Wazeba AR 1–1a; Munro-Hay 1984, p. 68)

Obv. Head and shoulders bust r., wearing headcloth. Disc and crescent at top. Ge'ez legend: **ወዘበ◡ነገሠ** (King WZB [Wazeba])

Rev. Small head and shoulders bust r., wearing headcloth, in circle. Disc and crescent at top. Ge'ez legend all round: **◡ ወዘበ ነገሠአከሰመ** (WZB Negus of Aksum).

Type 18 reads only: **◡ ነገሠአከሰመ** (Negus of Aksum).

The letter G may face right or left.

21	1989–5–18–38	0.48	12:00	Type 17
22	1989–5–18–39	0.82	12:00	
23	1989–5–18–40	0.80	12:00	
24	1969–6–24–6	0.72	12:00	

Wazeba/Ousanas
Silver
Type 19 (Wazeba/Ousanas bi-regnal issue AR 1; Munro-Hay 1984, p. 66)

Obv. As Type 17 (Wazeba AR 1) obv. Sometimes dots flank the disc and crescent.

Rev. As Type 28 (Ousanas AR 3) rev.

25	1989–5–18–37	0.78	12:00	

Ousanas
Gold
Types 20–24 (Type 20, Ousanas AV 1; Munro-Hay 1984, p. 56; variants Type 21, AV 1a; Type 22, AV 1b, Munro-Hay 1984, pp. 57–8; Type 23, AV 1c, Munro-Hay 1986, MH 26 (J-J 112); Type 24, AV 1d, Juel-Jensen 1994, J-J 403)

Obv. Half-length bust r., crowned, holding spear, between two wheat-stalks. Disc and crescent at top. Greek legend: OYCANACB◡ACIΛY C (Ki[n]g Ousanas).

Rev. As obv. but wearing headcloth and holding branch/fly-whisk (?): AξWMITWNBI◡CIΓICENE (Of the Aksumites man of Gisene) – WM and WN are written as monograms.

The variants have minor differences in the arrangement of the legend, and insert the Ɛ missing on the obverse legend: OYCANACB◡ACIΛƐ YC.

Type 21 (AV 1a) has the same reverse arrangement as Type 20.

Type 22 (AV 1b) has the reverse legend: AξWMITWNB◡ICIΓICENE, and includes a star-like symbol above the king's head.

Type 23 (AV 1c) is apparently a combination of the obverse of Type 21 with a reverse which has the same legend form as Type 22 but lacks the star symbol.

Type 24 (AV 1d) has the obverse legend: OYCANACB◡ACIΛƐ YC, and the reverse legend: AξWMITWNBI◡CIΓICENE.

26	1925–11–12–1	2.56	12:00	Type 20 (AV 1)

Ousanas
Silver
Type 25 (Ousanas AR 1; Munro-Hay 1984, p. 59)

Obv. Head and shoulders bust r., wearing headcloth. Disc and crescent at top. Greek legend all round: OYCANAC◡BACIΛƐYC (King Ousanas).

Rev. As obv.: BCΛCI (or BICICΛC) ◡AξWMITWN (K[in]g of the Aksumites).

Ousanas
Silver
Type 26 (Ousanas AR 2; Munro-Hay 1984, p. 60)

Obv. Head and shoulders bust r., wearing headcloth. Disc and crescent at top. Greek legend all round: OYCANAC◡BACIΛƐYC (King Ousanas).

Rev. As obv.: ◡AξWMITWNBICIΓICENE (Of the Aksumites man of Gisene), occasionally written ◡AξWMTWN . . . or BCI . . . or BICIΓICCN with the N reversed.

27	1969–6–24–3	2.11	12:00	The last letter of the rev. legend is lacking
28	1989–5–18–15	2.00	12:00	The first I of BICI is lacking

Ousanas

Silver

Type 27 (Ousanas AR 4; Munro-Hay 1984, p. 62; J-J 308)

Obv. Head and shoulders bust r., wearing headcloth. Disc and crescent at top. Greek legend: OYCANAC⌣BACIΛƐYC (King Ousanas).

Rev. Head and shoulders bust r., wearing headcloth. Disc and crescent at top. Greek legend all round: AξWMITWNBICIΓICENE (Of the Aksumites man of Gisene).

Ousanas

Silver

Type 28 (Ousanas AR 3; Munro-Hay 1984, p. 61)

Obv. Head and shoulders bust r., wearing headcloth. Disc and crescent at top. Greek legend: AξWMITWN (Of the Aksumites).

Rev. Small head and shoulders bust r., wearing headcloth, in circle. Area inside circle gilt on many examples. Disc and crescent at top, sometimes flanked with an extra dot on each side. Greek legend all round: ⌣OYCANACBACIΛƐYC (King Ousanas), or in one case OYANA.

The letter N may occasionally be reversed.

29	1969–6–24–4	0.85	12:00
30	1989–5–18–16	0.60	12:00
31	1989–5–18–17	0.71	12:00
32	1989–5–18–18	0.64	12:00
33	1989–5–18–19	0.61	12:00
34	1989–5–18–20	0.51	12:00
35	1989–5–18–21	0.79	12:00
36	1989–5–18–22	0.70	12:00
37	1989–5–18–24	0.80	12:00
38	1989–5–18–25	0.43	12:00
39	1989–5–18–26	0.77	11:00

Ousanas

Bronze

Type 29 (Ousanas AE 1; Munro-Hay 1984, p. 63)

Obv. Head and shoulders bust r., wearing headcloth, flanked by two wheat-stalks. Disc and crescent at top. Greek legend: OYCANAC⌣BACIΛƐYC (King Ousanas), or in one case (Munro-Hay 1986, 25) YCANAC⌣BACIΛƐYCO.

Rev. Head and shoulders bust to r., wearing headcloth, within two circles. Greek legend: Aξ+ WMI ([Of the] Aksumi[tes]). What the little cross in the legend represents is uncertain.

40	1969–6–24–5	1.23	12:00

Ousanas

Bronze

Type 30 (Ousanas AE 2; Munro-Hay 1984, p. 64)

Obv. As Type 29 (Ousanas AE 1) obv.

Rev. Head and shoulders bust r., wearing headcloth, in circle. Outer striated border circle. Greek legend: OYC ANA (Ousana).

This coin is important in that it links the pagan Ousanas with the Ousana(s) without religious symbol issues, having an obverse the same as Type 29 and a reverse the same as the obverse of Type 33.

Ousanas

Bronze

Type 31 (Ousanas AE 3; not in Munro-Hay 1984. Identical to AR 2)

Obv. and rev. identical to Ousanas AR 2, Type 26.

41	1869–1–1–3	1.69	Obverse surface perished

Ousana(s) without religious symbol

Silver

Types 32–33 (Ousana without religious symbol AR 1; Munro-Hay 1984, p. 65)

Obv. Head and shoulders bust r., wearing headcloth, in two circles. Outer striated border circle. Greek legend: Type 32 (very rare), OYC ANAC (Ousanas); Type 33, OYC ANA (Ousana) or sometimes OΛC ANA, OAC AHA and variants.

Rev. As obv.: BAC IΛƐI (or variants IΛƐY, IΛƐΛ, IΛCI).

42	1989–5–18–32	0.90	12:00	Type 32; legend obv.: OVC ANAC; rev.: BACI ΛƐYC
43	1969–6–24–13	1.26	12:00	
44	1969–6–24–14	0.67	12:00	
45	1989–5–18–28	1.26	12:00	
46	1989–5–18–29	0.67	12:00	
47	1989–5–18–30	1.01	12:00	
48	1989–5–18–31	1.46	12:00	
49	1989–5–18–33	1.03	12:00	
50	1989–5–18–34	0.70	12:00	
51	1989–5–18–35	0.76	12:00	

Ousana without religious symbol

Bronze

Type 34 (Juel-Jensen 1986, pp. 255–6; J-J 152)

Obv. Head and shoulders bust r., wearing headcloth, in two circles. Greek legend: OΛC ANA (Ousana).

Rev. As obv.: BAC IΛƐY (King).

Obv. and rev are in fact the same as Type 33 above, including one of the reverse legend variants.

Juel-Jensen suggested that Type 30 (Munro-Hay 1986, p. 19, coll. no. MH 25a) was another example of this coin, but in fact the wheat-stalks on the obverse of Type 30 are visible.

EZANA(S), BEFORE HIS CONVERSION TO CHRISTIANITY IN *c.* AD 330

Ezanas
Gold

Types 35–37 (Ezanas pagan AV 1, 1a, 1b; Munro-Hay 1984, pp. 70–71)

Obv. Half-length bust r., crowned, holding spear, between two wheat-stalks. Disc and crescent at top, sometimes flanked by dots. Greek legend: Types 35–6 (AV 1–1a), HZANACBᴗACIΛΕ YC; Type 37 (AV 1b), HZANACBAᴗCIΛΕ YC (King Ezanas).

A further variant Type 37i (Juel-Jensen 1985, J-J 64) has the legend HZANACB.AᴗCIΛΕ YC, and the spear which the king holds is beaded.

Rev. As obv. but wearing headcloth and holding branch or fly-whisk (?) and with sometimes a dot or group of dots over the head: AξWMITWNᴗBICIAʻΛΕN Ɛ (Type 36 (1a), AξWMITWNB'ᴗᴵᴄIAʻΛΕNΕ) (Of the Aksumites man of Alene).

| 52 | 1989–5–18–41 | 1.84 | 12:00 | Type 36 (AV 1a) |

Ezanas
Gold

Type 38 (Ezanas pagan AV 2; Munro-Hay 1984, p. 74)

Obv. Head and shoulders bust r., disc and crescent at top. Greek legend, mostly illegible: .A.ᴗZI. (King?).
Rev. Wheat-stalk in centre field. Greek legend: MΣA NAC (Ezanas).

The type is known only from a modern forgery (Munro-Hay, Oddy and Cowell 1988, SG. 617) based on Type 41.

Ezanas
Silver

Type 39 (Ezanas pagan AR 1; Munro-Hay 1984, p. 72)

Obv. Head and shoulders bust r., wearing headcloth. Disc and crescent at top, sometimes flanked with dots. Greek legend: HZAᴗNAC (Ezanas).
Rev. Similar small bust in circle. Area inside circle sometimes gilt. Disc and crescent as obv. Greek legend all round: ᴗBACIΛΕYC (King).

53	1989–5–18–23	0.80	12:00
54	1989–5–18–27	0.40	12:00
55	1968–4–1–3	0.53	12:00
56	1989–5–18–42	0.43	12:00
57	1989–5–18–43	0.59	12:00

58	1989–5–18–44	0.44	12:00
59	1989–5–18–46	0.30	12:00
60	1989–5–18–47	0.32	12:00
61	1989–5–18–48	0.26	12:00
62	1989–5–18–49	0.54	12:00
63	1989–5–18–50	0.43	12:00
64	1989–5–18–52	0.52	12:00
65	1989–5–18–53	0.45	12:00
66	1989–5–18–54	0.33	12:00

Ezanas
Bronze

Type 40 (Ezanas pagan AE 1; Munro-Hay 1984, p. 73; J-J 154)

Obv. and rev. as Type 39 (Ezanas pagan AR 1) without gilding.

Ezanas
Bronze

Type 41 (Ezanas pagan AE 2; Munro-Hay 1984, p. 74)

Obv. Head and shoulders bust r., in two concentric circles. Greek legend: BACI ΛΕYC (King), sometimes BACI ΛΕYᴄ (BᴧᴄI ᴧCVC).
Rev. Wheat-stalk in centre field. Disc and crescent at top (missing on some examples). Greek legend: HZAᴗNAC (Ezanas).

| 67 | 1914–8–10–8 | 0.82 | 6:00 |
| 68 | 1926–1–8–82 | 0.55 | 8:00 |

Ezanas without religious symbol
Silver

Type 42 (Ezanas without religious symbol AR 1; Munro-Hay 1984, p. 75)

Obv. Head and shoulders bust r., wearing headcloth, in one or two concentric circles. Greek legend: HZA NAC (Ezanas).
Rev. As obv.: BACI ΛΕYC (King), sometimes BAC ΛΕᴧC, BAC VCΛ.

| 69 | 1989–5–18–36 | 0.74 | 12:00 |
| 70 | 1968–4–1–2 | 0.74 | 12:00 |

Ezanas without religious symbol
Silver

Type 43 (Ezanas without religious symbol AR 1a; Munro-Hay 1984, p. 76)

Obv. Head and shoulders bust to r., wearing headcloth, in a circle. Small gilt circle with four lines radiating from it at top, between the inner circle and a second outer circle. Greek legend: HZA NAC (Ezanas).

Rev. Similar smaller bust in circle. Greek legend: BACI ΛΕΥC (King).

71	1989–5–18–45	0.66	12:00
72	1989–5–18–51	0.82	12:00

Ezanas without religious symbol
Bronze

Type 44 (Ezanas without religious symbol AE 1; Munro-Hay 1984, p. 77)

Obv. and rev. as Type 42 (Ezanas without religious symbol AR 1) with similar variants in the reverse legend: BAC ΛΕΛC, BΛCΛ CY.

73	1969–6–24–7	1.21	12:00

Anonymous without religious symbol
Gold

Type 45 (Anonymous without religious symbol AV 1; Munro-Hay 1984, p. 78)

Obv. and rev. as Type 42 rev.

The type is certainly a forgery (Tringali 1973, 2).

Anonymous without religious symbol
Silver

Type 46 (Anonymous without religious symbol AR 1; Munro-Hay 1984, p. 78)

Obv. and rev. as Type 42 rev.

The Early Christian Period, *c.* AD 340–540

EZANA(S), AFTER HIS CONVERSION TO CHRISTIANITY IN *c.* AD 330

Ezanas
Gold

Type 47 (Ezanas Christian AV 1; Munro-Hay 1984, p. 81)

Obv. Half-length bust r., crowned, holding stick or sceptre, flanked by two wheat-stalks sometimes with a dot at the apex, the whole in a beaded circle. The bust is thus more compressed than for the AV of Aphilas, Wazeba and Ousanas. Greek legend all round with crosses at top, bottom and both sides: ✠HZA✠NAC✠BACI✠ΛΕYC (King Ezanas).

Rev. As obv., but wearing headcloth and holding branch (?): ✠AξW✠MITWN✠BICI✠AʹΛΕNΕ (Of the Aksumites man of Alene).

Letter forms often simplified; C (square in form) represents C, Ε or B, H for H and N; Λ for Λ and A.

74	1921–3–16–1	1.93	1:00

Ezanas
Bronze

Type 48 (Ezanas Christian AE 1; Munro-Hay 1984, p. 83)

Obv. Head and shoulders bust r., wearing headcloth. Cross at top. Greek legend: HZA✠NAC (Ezanas).

Rev. As obv. Legend indistinct, perhaps: BACI ΛΕYC (King).

Ezana
Gold

Type 49 (Ezana Christian AV 1; Munro-Hay 1984, p. 84)

Obv. As Type 47 (Ezanas Christian AV 1) except that the dot above the head is sometimes replaced by a letter, symbol or combination of dots. Greek legend all round: ✠HZA✠NAB✠ACI✠ΛΕY (Kin[g] Ezana).

Rev. As Type 47 (Ezanas Christian AV 1) except that a stick sometimes appears instead of the branch. Greek legend all round: ✠AξW✠MITB✠ICI✠AΛHN (Of the Aksumites man of Alen).

Letter variations, even partially retrograde legends, are found.

75	1915–1–8–81	1.45	12:00

Anonymous

Silver

Type 50 (Anonymous AR 2; Munro-Hay 1984, p. 86)

Obv. Head and shoulders bust r., wearing headcloth, in a circle. Greek legend: BAX ACA often CΛX ΛCΛ (Ba<u>kh</u>asa) – interpretation uncertain – sometimes BAX ΛBΛ, even CΛX IΛC Λ.

Rev. Greek cross in circle centre field, the cross voided and inlaid with gold. Greek legend all round: TOYTOAPECHTHXWPA (May this please the country) written TOVTOΛPCCHTHXWPΛ *et var.*; sometimes TOTYO . . . or retrograde.

76	1968–4–1–4	0.89	12:00	TOTYO . . .
77	1989–5–18–55	0.72	12:00	
78	1989–5–18–56	0.74	12:00	
79	1989–5–18–57	0.75	3:00	
80	1989–5–18–58	0.84	12:00	
81	1989–5–18–59	0.87	12:00	
82	1989–5–18–60	0.71	1:00	

Anonymous

Bronze

Types 51–52 (Anonymous AE 1; Munro-Hay 1984, p. 87)

Obv. Head and shoulders bust r., wearing headcloth, with the legend in two parts broken by the king's head, in a circle (or sometimes two). Greek legend: BACI ΛEYC (King), often written CΛCI ΛCVC.

Variants read BACI ΛYC, BAC ΛCYC.

Rev. Greek cross in a circle, usually solid with flared equal-length arms but sometimes open (e.g. 136, 141, 149). Greek legend all round: TOYTOAPECHTHXWPA (May this please the country). A number of variants, incomplete legends, and differences in style are found. Sometimes an outer circle is also visible, or even two (e.g. 141).

There is a 'miniature' or copy version, Type 51, of this issue, recorded from finds in Egypt and other places.

Die-axes vary

83	1926–1–8–83	0.55	Type 51
84	Jan.1919 MIN	0.58	
85	OR 3503	0.43	
86	OR 3504	0.82	
87	1888–10–8–2	0.78	
88	1888–10–8–3	0.41	
89	1888–10–8–4	0.41	
91	OR 3501	0.61	
90	1868–12–42–1	1.11	Found near Lake Ashangi. Type 52
92	1953–2–15–15	0.72	
93	1953–4–2–14	1.53	
94	1953–4–2–16	0.88	
95	1953–4–2–17	0.40	
96	1953–4–2–18	0.92	

97	1953–4–2–19	0.74
98	1888–10–8–1	0.91
99	1953–4–2–20	1.08
100	1989–5–18–61	1.06
101	1989–5–18–62	1.60
102	1989–5–18–63	1.15
103	1989–5–18–64	1.12
104	1989–5–18–65	0.81
105	1989–5–18–66	0.66
106	1989–5–18–67	1.05
107	1989–5–18–68	1.11
108	1989–5–18–69	0.93
109	1989–5–18–70	1.03
110	1989–5–18–71	1.30
111	1989–5–18–72	0.97
112	1989–5–18–73	1.18
113	1989–5–18–74	1.22
114	1989–5–18–75	0.84
115	1989–5–18–76	0.87
116	1989–5–18–77	0.88
117	1989–5–18–78	0.88
118	1989–5–18–79	1.65
119	1989–5–18–80	1.06
120	1989–5–18–81	1.35
121	1989–5–18–82	1.31
122	1989–5–18–83	1.06
123	1989–5–18–84	1.57
124	1989–5–18–85	1.81
125	1989–5–18–86	1.30
126	1989–5–18–87	1.29
127	1989–5–18–88	0.83
128	1989–5–18–89	0.98
129	1989–5–18–90	0.77
130	1989–5–18–91	0.32
131	1989–5–18–92	0.67
132	1989–5–18–93	1.20
133	1989–5–18–94	1.16
134	1989–5–18–95	1.43
135	1989–5–18–96	0.72
136	1989–5–18–97	1.08
137	1989–5–18–98	1.51
138	1989–5–18–99	0.93
139	1989–5–18–100	1.12
140	1989–5–18–101	1.29
141	1989–5–18–102	1.42
142	1989–5–18–103	1.39
143	1989–5–18–104	1.66
144	1989–5–18–105	1.27
145	1989–5–18–106	1.43
146	1989–5–18–107	0.93
147	1989–5–18–108	0.94
148	1989–5–18–109	1.25
149	1989–5–18–110	0.30
150	1989–5–18–111	1.53
151	1989–5–18–112	1.23
152	1989–5–18–113	0.53
153	1989–5–18–114	1.49

154	1989–5–18–115	0.75
155	1989–5–18–116	0.67
156	1989–5–18–117	0.71
157	1989–5–18–118	1.11
158	1989–5–18–119	1.33
159	1989–5–18–120	1.29
160	1989–5–18–121	0.53
161	1989–5–18–122	1.18
162	1989–5–18–123	1.21
163	1989–5–18–124	1.36
164	1989–5–18–125	0.80
165	1989–5–18–126	1.29
166	1989–5–18–127	1.75
167	1989–5–18–128	1.01
168	1989–5–18–129	1.24
169	1989–5–18–130	1.44
170	1989–5–18–131	1.36
171	1989–5–18–132	1.17
172	1989–5–18–133	1.59
173	1989–5–18–134	0.65
174	1989–5–18–135	1.08
175	1989–5–18–136	1.32
176	1989–5–18–137	1.27
177	1989–5–18–138	0.94
178	1989–5–18–139	0.73
179	1989–5–18–140	0.88
180	1989–5–18–141	1.81
181	1989–5–18–142	0.85
182	1989–5–18–143	1.50
183	1989–5–18–144	1.04
184	1989–5–18–145	1.21
185	1989–5–18–146	0.86
186	1989–5–18–147	0.83
187	1989–5–18–148	1.18
188	1989–5–18–149	1.24
189	1989–5–18–150	1.03
190	1989–5–18–151	1.03
191	1989–5–18–152	0.42
192	1989–5–18–153	0.55
193	1989–5–18–154	1.01
194	1989–5–18–155	1.49
195	1989–5–18–156	1.15
196	1989–5–18–157	0.97
197	1989–5–18–158	0.78
197a	1989–5–18–159	0.82
198	1989–5–18–160	1.22
199	1989–5–18–161	0.94
200	1989–5–18–162	0.91
201	1989–5–18–163	0.48
202	1989–5–18–164	1.20
203	1989–5–18–165	0.62
204	1989–5–18–166	1.20
205	1989–5–18–167	1.12
206	1989–5–18–168	1.13
207	1989–5–18–169	0.82
208	1989–5–18–170	1.08
209	1989–5–18–171	1.20
210	1989–5–18–172	1.10
211	1989–5–18–173	0.98
212	1989–5–18–174	0.83
213	1989–5–18–175	1.05
214	1989–5–18–176	1.32
215	1989–5–18–177	1.15
216	1989–5–18–178	0.97
217	1989–5–18–179	1.26
218	1989–5–18–180	1.16
219	1989–5–18–181	1.20
220	1989–5–18–182	0.83
221	1989–5–18–183	0.65
222	1989–5–18–184	0.75
223	1989–5–18–185	0.90
224	1989–5–18–186	0.72
225	1989–5–18–187	0.88
226	1989–5–18–188	0.42
227	1989–5–18–189	1.10
228	1989–5–18–190	0.88
229	1989–5–18–191	1.10
230	1989–5–18–192	0.92
231	1989–5–18–193	1.26
232	1989–5–18–194	1.21
233	1989–5–18–195	1.07
234	1989–5–18–196	0.65
235	1989–5–18–197	0.90
236	1989–5–18–198	1.49
237	1989–5–18–199	1.61
238	1989–5–18–200	0.96
239	1989–5–18–201	1.14
240	1989–5–18–202	1.76
241	1989–5–18–203	0.69
242	1989–5–18–204	1.34
243	1989–5–18–205	0.86
244	1989–5–18–206	1.26

Anonymous

Bronze

Type 53 (Anonymous AE 1.5; Juel-Jensen 1991, p. 39; J-J 251)

Obv. Apparently as Type 50 above.

Rev. Cross with flared arms, with a central punch-hole inlaid with gold, framed by two wheat-stalks in the centre field. The wheat-stalks have stems which divide the legend at the bottom. Greek legend: TOYTOAPECHTHXWPA (May this please the country). In the only known example of this coin the legend is retrograde, reading clockwise from the top TYOTAPWX HTHCCPAO.

Ouazebas

Bronze

Types 54–58 (Ouazebas AE 1–1a; Munro-Hay 1984, pp. 91–2: Type 56, with the obv. legend on both sides; West 1987, p. 39)

Obv. Head and shoulders bust r., flanked by two wheat-stalks. Cross at top. Greek legend all round: ✠OYAZEBACBACIΛEYC (King Ouazebas). A variant Type 57 reads ✠COYAZHBACBACIΛEY; another variant (J-J 382), Type 57i, reads ✠OYAZHAC.

Rev. Similar small bust in circle. Area inside circle gilt. Cross at top. Greek legend all round: ✠TOYTOAPECHTHXWPA (May this please the country). Variant Type 58 reads ✠HTHXWPATOYTOAPEC. Type 55 has apparently the word (BA)CI (ΛE)VC (King) written inside the inner circle (Anzani 1926, 79a–80).

Many letter variants occur, some being written backwards, or upside down.

245	1969–6–24–8	1.95	12:00	
246	1976–10–16–2	1.12	12:00	
247	1868–12–19–1	2.12	12:00	
248	1989–5–18–208	2.33	12:00	
249	1989–5–18–209	1.42	12:00	
250	1989–5–18–210	1.94	12:00	
251	1989–5–18–211	2.28	11:00	
252	1989–5–18–212	1.83	12:00	
253	1989–5–18–213	1.23	12:00	
254	1989–5–18–214	1.94	12:00	
255	1989–5–18–215	1.96	12:00	
256	1989–5–18–216	2.55	12:00	
257	1989–5–18–217	1.69	12:00	
258	1989–5–18–219	1.70	12:00	
259	1989–5–18–220	1.60	12:00	
260	1989–5–18–221	1.99	12:00	
261	1989–5–18–222	0.82	12:00	
262	1989–5–18–223	1.53	12:00	
263	1989–5–18–225	1.80	12:00	
264	1989–5–18–226	1.52	12:00	
265	1989–5–18–227	0.79	12:00	
266	1989–5–18–228	1.50	12:00	
267	1989–5–18–229	2.04	12:00	
268	1989–5–18–230	1.74	12:00	
269	1989–5–18–231	1.38	12:00	
270	1989–5–18–232	1.09	11:00	
271	1989–5–18–233	0.87	12:00	
272	1989–5–18–234	1.53	12:00	TOTYO
273	1989–5–18–236	1.89	12:00	
274	1989–5–18–237	2.64	12:00	
275	1989–5–18–239	2.04	12:00	
276	1989–5–18–240	1.86	12:00	
277	1989–5–18–241	1.66	11:00	
278	1989–5–18–242	1.79	1:00	
279	1989–5–18–243	1.29	12:00	
280	1989–5–18–244	0.82	12:00	
281	1989–5–18–245	1.47	12:00	
282	1989–5–18–246	1.73	11:00	
283	1989–5–18–247	1.83	12:00	
284	1989–5–18–248	1.10	12:00	

285	1989–5–18–207	2.23	12:00	Type 57 obv. leg. variant
286	1989–5–18–224	1.54	12:00	Type 57 obv. leg. variant
287	1989–5–18–218	2.07	12:00	Type 58 rev. leg. variant
288	1989–5–18–235	2.35	12:00	Type 58 rev. leg. variant
289	1989–5–18–238	1.82	1:00	Type 58 rev. leg. variant

Eon
Gold

Types 59–62 (Eon AV 1, 1a, 1b, 1c; Munro-Hay 1984, pp. 88–9)

Obv. Head and shoulders bust r., crowned, usually holding short stick (or very rarely branch/fly-whisk?), flanked by two wheat-stalks, in a beaded circle. Greek legend all round, starting at different places on different examples: ✠CAC✠CIN✠CAX✠ACA (on a few pieces – including 290 below – distinctly written letters have established the most probable reading as ✠BAC✠CIN✠BAX✠ACA, but the interpretation remains uncertain). On these and many subsequent types the letters B, E and C appear as C (square in form), and A and Λ appear as Λ.

A variety Type 60 (1a) reads (sometimes with letters reversed): ✠CAC✠CAC✠ACA✠XAC; other varieties are Type 61 (AV 1b), ✠CYC✠CIN✠CAX✠ACA; Type 62 (AV 1c), ✠CAC✠ACA✠XAC✠CAC

Rev. As obv. but wearing headcloth and usually holding branch/fly-whisk (?), or short stick/sceptre. Greek legend all round: ✠EWN✠BIC✠IAN✠AAΦ (Eon Bisi Anaaph). The varieties Type 61 (1b) and Type 62 (1c) read: ✠IAN✠IWC✠XAΛ✠BIC. The N is often drawn in the Ge'ez style, and Φ may appear as X.

290	1915–1–8–78	1.43	10:00	Type 59 (AV 1)
291	1908–10–6–6	1.53	10:00	Type 59 (AV 1)

Anonymous
Gold

Type 63 (Anonymous AV 1; Munro-Hay 1984, p. 90)

Obv. As Eon; the king sometimes holding a short stick: ✠CIN✠CAX✠ACA✠CAC and variants (interpretation uncertain). One type with the legend ✠CAC✠INƆ✠CAX✠ACA CA also has the symbol ⵕ above the head.

Rev. As Eon: ✠CYN✠CAX✠ACA✠CAC and variants (interpretation uncertain).

292	OR 3505	1.55	12:00

Types 64–65. These are silver and bronze casts of Type 63, presumably modern forgeries.

Anonymous (?)
Silver

Type 66 (Juel-Jensen 1993, pp. 3–4; J-J 300)

Obv. Half-length bust r., crowned, holding cross on staff. Cross behind head. Ge'ez legend: ነገሠበንስአ··አ (King B<u>H</u>SA . . . A?). The last letter might be a cross? The name could perhaps parallel the so far uninterpreted Greek group BAX ACA found on a number of other issues.

- *Rev.* Cross on stand in centre field, flanked by two wheat-stalks linked to the stand at the base by a ribbon. Ge'ez le·gend: አ··አበሐረበከለ (From God's side we have it).

Type 67 is a gold type of M<u>H</u>DYS (the vocalisation of the name is unknown), recently published (Munro-Hay 1995); its design is completely different from any other Aksumite gold coin yet known, but weight, size and gold content appear to conform to the Aksumite pattern and to testify in favour of its authenticity.

Type 68 is a gold cast of the silver Type 69, and is presumably a modern forgery; Munro-Hay 1984, p. 93.

M<u>H</u>DYS
Silver

Type 69 (M<u>H</u>DYS AR 1; Munro-Hay 1984, p. 93; J-J 247)

Obv. Half-length bust r., crowned, holding cross on staff. Cross behind head. Ge'ez legend:
ነገሠ : መወአ : መሐደየስ (The victorious King M<u>H</u>DYS).

Rev. Cross on stand in centre field, flanked by two wheat-stalks joined to the stand at the base. Dot between apex of wheat-stalks. Ge'ez legend:
በዘ : መሰቀለ : ተመወአ (By this cross he will conquer).

M<u>H</u>DYS
Bronze

Type 70 (M<u>H</u>DYS AE 1; Munro-Hay 1984, p. 94)

Obv. Head and shoulders bust r., wearing headcloth, flanked by two wheat-stalks. Cross at top. Ge'ez legend: መሐደየስነጘገሠአከሰመ (M<u>H</u>DYS King of Aksum).

Rev. Greek cross, with a punch-hole inlaid with gold, in a circle in the centre field. Ge'ez legend:
በዘመወአስመሰቀለ (By this cross he will conquer).

Rarely, separation marks : between the words may appear. A rare variant, Type 70i, lacks the cross before the reverse legend.

Numerous examples have been overstruck by Type 76 (Anonymous AE 2).

Die-axes vary

293	1925–9–2–1	1.08
294	1953–4–2–7	1.08
295	1989–5–18–249	0.95
296	1989–5–18–250	1.47
297	1989–5–18–251	1.19
298	1989–5–18–252	1.25
299	1989–5–18–253	0.67
300	1989–5–18–254	0.69
301	1989–5–18–255	1.03
302	1989–5–18–256	1.06

Ebana
Gold

Types 71–72 (Ebana AV 1, AV 1a; Munro-Hay 1984, pp. 95–6).

These coins constitute by far the commonest of all Aksumite gold types.

Obv. As Eon, but with a variety of letters and symbols above head: ✠CIN✠CAX✠ACA✠CAC and variants (interpretation uncertain). The variety Type 72 reads ✠CAC✠CAC✠ACA✠XAC.

Rev. As Eon, but often dot above head, and with legend: ✠ANA✠BAC✠ACA✠CEB = EB✠ANA✠BAC✠(I)ΛEY✠C (Ki[n]g Ebana).

Letters may be unclear (as with many issues of this period and later in Aksum the Greek is debased, with Λ for Λ and A; C for C, B or E), or reversed, or upside down.

303	1904–4–4–1	1.58	12:00	with H obv.
304	1870–3–1–1	1.54	11:00	
305	1915–1–8–79	1.56	12:00	with Λ obv.
306	1872–5–7–1	1.59	12:00	
307	1925–8–5–1	1.57	12:00	Type 72 (AV 1a)
308	1989–5–18–257	1.63	12:00	

Anonymous (=Ebana)
Gold

Type 73 (Anonymous AV 3; Munro-Hay 1984, p. 98)
Obv. and rev. as Ebana AV 1: rev. legend:
✠ANA✠CAC✠ACA✠CAC. The type is an incorrectly engraved die for Ebana.

Ebana
Silver

Type 74 (Ebana AR 1; Munro-Hay 1984, p. 97)

Obv. Head and shoulders bust r., crowned, in beaded circle. Greek legend: EB ANA (Ebana).

Rev. Central lozenge inlaid with gold, with four crosses attached to the extremities, forming a cross-crosslet with the letters of the legend interspersed between them. Greek legend: ✠BC✠ΛC✠IΛ✠ƐY (King) and rare variants (e.g. Munro-Hay 1986, 99) – but the spelling is always incorrect. Many are overstruck on Type 50 (Anonymous AR 2) pieces.

Die-axes vary

309	1968–4–1–5	0.86	Overstruck on Type 50
310	1915–2–5–2	0.67	
311	1989–5–18–258	0.61	
312	1989–5–18–259	0.60	
313	1989–5–18–260	0.77	
314	1989–5–18–261	0.65	
315	1989–5–18–262	0.64	

Type 75 is a bronze version of Type 74; one example has so far been recorded: Munro-Hay 1984, p. 97.

Anonymous

Bronze

Type 76 (Anonymous AE 2; Munro-Hay 1984, p. 99)

Obv. Half-length bust to r., crowned, holding hand-cross which usually breaks the legend on the right. Rarely cross (e.g. 347) or letter A at top; usually a cross occurs in the legend or behind the head on the left balancing the hand-cross. Greek legend: BAX(✠) A CΛ (interpretation uncertain), often appearing as CΛXX Λ CΛ.

Rev. Greek cross with punch-hole inlaid with gold; the arms of the cross touch or merge with an inner circle. Greek legend all round: TOYTOAPECHTHXWPA (May this please the country). There are sometimes errors, e.g. TOTYO. . ., TOVOT. . ., in the writing of the legend, which may also be retrograde, or with some reversed letters; or the legend may be nonsense (e.g. 358, TOTV. . .CV✠WΛOIV.

Die-axes vary

316	1953–4–2–9	1.12
317	1953–4–2–10	0.90
318	1953–4–2–11	1.12
319	1953–4–2–12	0.85
320	1953–4–2–13	0.86
321	1935–4–1–11249	0.93
322	1880–6–4–30	0.80
323	1896–1–1–2	0.78
324	1969–6–1–10	1.17
325	1969–6–24–11	0.84
326	1989–5–18–263	0.50
327	1989–5–18–264	0.63
328	1989–5–18–265	1.19
329	1989–5–18–266	1.29
330	1989–5–18–267	1.18
331	1989–5–18–268	0.80
332	1989–5–18–269	1.33
333	1989–5–18–270	0.37
334	1989–5–18–271	1.05
335	1989–5–18–272	0.98
336	1989–5–18–273	1.13
337	1989–5–18–274	1.35
338	1989–5–18–275	1.00
339	1989–5–18–276	1.50
340	1989–5–18–277	0.81
341	1989–5–18–278	1.06
342	1989–5–18–279	1.40
343	1989–5–18–280	0.97
344	1989–5–18–281	0.77
345	1989–5–18–282	0.89
346	1989–5–18–283	1.04
347	1989–5–18–284	1.00
348	1989–5–18–285	1.02
349	1989–5–18–286	1.43
350	1989–5–18–287	0.73
351	1989–5–18–288	1.52
352	1989–5–18–289	1.07
353	1989–5–18–290	0.90
354	1989–5–18–291	0.80
355	1989–5–18–292	1.00
356	1989–5–18–293	0.82
357	1989–5–18–294	0.54
358	1989–5–18–295	0.72
359	1989–5–18–296	1.11
360	1989–5–18–297	0.90
361	1989–5–18–298	1.02
362	1989–5–18–299	1.25
363	1989–5–18–300	1.38
364	1989–5–18–301	1.26
365	1989–5–18–302	1.30
366	1989–5–18–303	1.14
367	1989–5–18–304	0.70
368	1989–5–18–305	0.67
369	1989–5–18–306	0.86
370	1989–5–18–307	1.02
371	1989–5–18–308	1.24
372	1989–5–18–309	0.88
373	1989–5–18–310	0.94
374	1989–5–18–311	1.01
375	1989–5–18–312	0.85
376	1989–5–18–313	0.70
377	1989–5–18–314	0.70
378	1989–5–18–315	0.78
379	1989–5–18–316	0.75
380	1989–5–18–317	0.72
381	1989–5–18–318	0.49
382	1989–5–18–319	0.79
383	1989–5–18–320	0.75
384	1989–5–18–321	0.55
385	1989–5–18–322	0.47
386	1989–5–18–323	0.81
387	1989–5–18–324	0.73
388	1989–5–18–325	1.12
389	1989–5–18–326	0.55
390	1989–5–18–327	0.83
391	1989–5–18–328	0.97
392	1989–5–18–329	1.46
393	1989–5–18–330	0.67
394	1989–5–18–331	0.87

395	1989–5–18–332	0.78
396	1989–5–18–333	0.96
397	1989–5–18–334	1.12
398	1989–5–18–335	0.62

Nezana

Gold

Type 77 (Nezana AV 1; Munro-Hay 1984, p. 108)

Obv. Half-length bust r., crowned, flanked by two wheat-stalks. Cross at top, with elongated stem reaching down to the king's head like a Latin cross. Greek legend all round: ✠ΝΕΖΑΝΑΒΑCΙΛΕΥC (King Nezana).

Rev. As obv. but wearing headcloth: ✠ΝΕΖΑΝΑΒΑCΙΛΕΥC (King Nezana).

Nezana

Gold

Type 78 (Nezana AV 2; Munro-Hay 1984, p. 109)

Obv. As Type 77 (Nezana AV 1) but Greek-style cross at top and Ge'ez letter **𐩬** by the king's chin. The king holds a short stick/sceptre: ✠CΝΙ✠CΑΧ✠ΑCΑ✠CΑC (interpretation uncertain).

Rev. As Type 77 (Nezana AV 1) rev.

Nezana

Gold

Type 79 (Nezana AV 3; Munro-Hay 1984, p. 110; J-J 196)

Obv. As Type 77 (Nezana AV 1) obv. but the king holds a short stick/sceptre, or the branch or fly-whisk, which divides the legend: ✠ΘΕΟΥΕ ΥΧΑΡΙCΤΙΑ (Thanks be to God).

Rev. As Type 77 (Nezana AV 1) rev., but sometimes the king holds a short, drooping stick.

Nezana

Gold

Type 79i (Nezana AV 4; Munro-Hay 1989, pp. 96–7)

Obv. As Type 77 (Nezana AV 1) obv.
Rev. As Type 81 (Anonymous AV 2) rev.

Nezana

Silver

Type 80 (Nezana AR 1; Munro-Hay 1984, p. 111)

Obv. Head and shoulders bust r. Ge'ez monogram NZWL at top. Greek legend: ΝΕΖΑ ΝΑΒΑ (K[ing?] Nezana).

Rev. As Type 88 (Ousanas AR 1) rev. Greek legend: ΘΕ ΟΥ ΧΛ ΠΙ (By the grace (?) of God) and variants.

Die-axes vary

399	1969–6–24–15	1.01
400	1989–5–18–339	1.10 The PI of the rev. legend is retrograde

Anonymous

Gold

Type 81 (Anonymous AV 2; Munro-Hay 1984, p. 112; J-J 384)

Obv. Half-length bust r., crowned, flanked by two wheat-stalks. Cross at top. One die has the Ge'ez letter **𐩬** near the king's chin. Greek legend all round: ✠CΝΙ✠CΑΧ✠ΑCΑ✠CΑC (✠CΝΙ✠CΑΧ✠ΛΧΛ✠CΛC. Interpretation uncertain). Die-linked with Type 78 (Nezana AV 2) and Type 83 (Nezool AV 2).

Rev. As obv. but wearing headcloth: ✠CΥΝ✠CΑΧ✠ΑCΑ✠CΑC (interpretation uncertain).

Nezool

Gold

Type 82 (Nezool AV 1; Munro-Hay 1984, pp. 113–14; J-J 197)

Obv. As Type 79 (Nezana AV 3) obv. The legend is broken by the fly-whisk or stick that the king holds at either ✠ΘΕΟΥΕ or ✠ΘΕΟΥ.

Rev. As Type 79 (Nezana AV 3) rev. but the king holds the fly-whisk or short, drooping stick. Greek legend: ✠ΒΑCΙΛ ΕΥCΝΕΖΟΩΛ or ✠ΒΑCΙΛΕ ΥCΝΕΖΟΩΛ (King Nezool), or sometimes with E instead of Ε.

401	1969–6–24–16	1.62	11:00

Nezool

Gold

Type 83 (Nezool AV 2; Munro-Hay 1984, p. 115)

Obv. As Type 78 (Nezana AV 2) obv.
Rev. As Type 82 (Nezool AV 1) rev.

Ousas

Gold

Types 84–85 (Type 84, Ousas AV 1; Munro-Hay 1984, p. 100. Type 85, Ousas AV 1a: Munro-Hay 1984, p. 101; J-J 9, 66)

Obv. Half-length bust r., crowned, holding stick, flanked by two wheat-stalks, in beaded inner circle. Crosses at top and bottom. Greek legend all round: ✠ΟΥCΑCΒ✠ΑCΙΛΕΥC (King Ousas).

Type 85 (AV 1a) lacks the second cross: ✠ΟΥCΑCΒΑCΙΛΕΥC. There is sometimes a small symbol by the left wheat-stalk.

Rev. As obv. but wearing headcloth and holding fly-whisk. There may be a dot above head. Greek legend all round: ⳨ΘΕΟΥΕΥΧΑΡΙCΤΙΑ (Thanks be to God). Letters may be upside down; V for A.

Ousas

Gold

Type 86 (Ousas AV 2; Munro-Hay 1984, p. 102)

Obv. Half-length bust r., crowned, holding branch/fly-whisk, flanked by two wheat-stalks. Cross at top. Greek legend: ⳨ΟΥCΑCΒ ΑCΙΛΕΥC (King Ousas).

Rev. As obv., but wearing headcloth and without branch/fly-whisk: ⳨ΘΕΟΥΙΑ ΕΥΧΑΡΙC (Thanks be to God) – legend (Theou eucharistia) garbled, the cross apparently acting as the letter T.

402   1989–5–18–336   1.62   12:00

Ousanas

Gold

Type 87 (Ousanas AV 1; Munro-Hay 1984, p. 103)

Obv. Half-length bust r., crowned, holding stick, flanked by two wheat-stalks, in beaded inner circle. Greek legend all round: ⳨ΟΥCΑΝΑCΒΑCΙΛΕΥC (King Ousanas). There is sometimes a small symbol by the left wheat-stalk.

Rev. As above but wearing headcloth and holding branch/fly-whisk. There may be a dot above head. Greek legend all round: ⳨ΘΕΟΥΕΥΧΑΡΙCΤΙΑ (Thanks be to God).

Letters may be upside down or reversed.

Ousanas

Silver

Type 88 (Ousanas AR 1; Munro-Hay 1984, p. 104)

Obv. Head and shoulders bust r., wearing headcloth. Cross at top. Greek legend: ⳨ΟΥCΑ ΝΑC (Ousanas) – the letter A may be upside down.

Rev. Greek cross touching outer border, with voided centre inlaid with gold, and small intermediate arms between the larger ones, which also separate the legend. Greek legend: B⟩ CI ⟨Ε YC, BY CI ΛΕ YC or BC CI ΛΕ YC (King).

Die-axes vary

403	1989–5–18–337	0.63	12:00	ΛΕ
404	1989–5–18–338	0.85	12:00	CI

Ousana

Gold

Types 89–90 (Type 89, Ousana AV 1, Munro-Hay 1984, pp. 105–6; J-J 78, 207. Type 90, Ousana AV 1a, Munro-Hay 1984, p. 107)

Obv. As Type 86 (Ousas AV 2) obv., but the king holds a short stick. Sometimes a symbol above the head (letter, dots). Greek legend: ⳨ΟΥCΑΝΑ B ΑCΙΛΕΥC (King Ousana). Letters may be reversed or upside down.

Type 90 (1a) shows the king holding a spear as well as the short stick, dividing the legend at ⳨ΟΥCΑΝ ΑB ΑCΙΛΕΥC; the king's crown is apparently of the older type with four elements instead of three, and the letter H appears above it.

Rev. As Type 86 (Ousas AV 2) rev. Sometimes holding stick or branch/fly-whisk (?): ⳨ΘΕΟΥΙΑ ΕΥΧΑΡΙC (By the grace of God), sometimes degenerated to BΕΟVΙ ΧΙΧΑΡΙC, and variants.

405   1969–6–24–12   1.57   12:00   Type 90 (AV 1a)

Kaleb

Gold

Types 91–96 (Type 91, Kaleb AV 1, Munro-Hay 1984, p. 116. Types 92–95, Kaleb AV 1a, 1b, 1c, 1d, Munro-Hay 1984, p. 117. Type 96, Kaleb AV 1e; Juel-Jensen 1988, p. 280; J-J 208).

Obv. Half-length bust r., crowned, holding stick, flanked by two wheat-stalks, in beaded inner circle. There is sometimes a small symbol by the left wheat-stalk. There may be a dot at the apex of the wheat-stalks. Ge'ez monogram KLB at top. Greek legend: ΧΑΛΗΒΒΑCΙΛΕΥC (King Khaleb).

Rev. As obv. but wearing headcloth and without dot or symbol. Ge'ez monogram KLB at top. Greek legend: ΥΙΟCΘΕΖΕΝΑ (Son of Thezena). Both legends may have many reversed letters.

Variants are distinguished by minor differences in the legend:
Type 92 (AV 1a), rev. legend Y⳨ΙΟCΘΕΖΕΝΑ
Type 93 (AV 1b), rev. legend ⳨ΥΙΟCΘΕΖΕΝΑ⳨
Type 94 (AV 1c), obv. legend ΧΑΛ⳨ΗΒΑ⳨CΙΛ⳨ΕΥC
Type 95 (AV 1d), rev. no monogram, legend ⳨ΥΙΟCΘΕΖΕΝΑ
Type 96 (AV 1e), obv. legend ΧΑΛ⳨ΗΒΒ⳨ΑCΙV⳨ΕVC; rev. as Type 95

406   1929–11–7–8   1.59   12:00   Type 95 (AV 1d)

Kaleb

Gold

Type 97 (Kaleb AV 2; Munro-Hay 1984, p. 118)

Obv. As Type 91 (Kaleb AV 1) obv., but with legend: ΧΑΛΗΒΒ⳨ΑCΙΛ⳨ΕΥC (King Khaleb).

Rev. As Type 87 (Ousanas AV 1) rev.

Kaleb

Gold

Types 98–109 (Type 98–99, Kaleb AV 3–3a, Munro-Hay

1984, p. 119. Type 100, Kaleb AV 3b, Munro-Hay 1984, p. 120. Types 101–102, Kaleb AV 3c(i)–3c(ii), Munro-Hay 1984, p. 121. Type 103, Kaleb AV 3c(iii), Juel-Jensen 1988, pp. 280–81, J-J 209. Types 104–107, Kaleb AV 3d–3g, Munro-Hay 1984, p. 122; Type 107, J-J 388. Type 108, Kaleb AV 3h, Munro-Hay 1984, p. 123. Type 109, Kaleb 3i; Juel-Jensen 1988, pp. 280–1; J-J 204.

Obv. As Type 91, but no monogram, and the legend: ✠ΧΑΛΗΒΒΑϹΙΛΕΥϹ (King Khaleb).

Rev. As Type 91, but no monogram, and the legend: ✠ΥΙΟϹΘΕΖΕΝΑϹ (?) (Son of Thezenas).

Variants (many letters are reversed or upside down; the letters A and Ε are hollow, without crossbars):

Type 99 (AV 3a), rev. legend ✠✠ΥΙΟϹΘΕΖΕΝΑ✠
Type 100 (AV 3b), rev. legend ✠ΥΙΟ✠ϹΘΕΖΕ✠ΝΑ
Type 101 (AV 3c(i)), obv. legend ✠ΧΑΗΒΒΑϹΙΛΕΥ✠; rev. legend ✠✠ΥΙΟϹΘΙΕΖΕΝΑ✠
Type 102 (AV 3c(ii)), obv. legend ✠ΧΑΗΒΒΑϹΙΛΕΥϹ
Type 103 (AV 3c(iii)), obv. legend ✠ΧΑΗΒΒ(ΑϹΙΛΕ?)VϹ✠; rev. legend ✠VΙΟ.ϹΘ ΕΖΕΝΑ=✠
Type 104 (AV 3d), rev. legend ✠✠ΥΙΟϹΘΙΕΖΕΝΑΟΥ✠
Type 105 (AV 3e), rev. legend ✠ΥΙΟϹΘΕΖΕΝΑ✠
Type 106 (AV 3f), rev. legend ✠✠ΥΙΟϹΘΕΖΕΝΑ✠
Type 107 (AV 3g), rev. legend ✠ΥΟΙ✠Ϲ ΘΕΖΕ✠ΝΑ
Type 108 (AV 3h), rev. legend ✠✠ΙΟϹΘΙΕΖΑΝΑΟΥΗ✠
Type 109 (AV 3i), obv. legend ✠ΧΑΗΒΒΑϹΙΛϹVϹΙ✠; rev. legend ✠✠ΛΙΟϹΟΙΕΝΕΝΑΟV✠

407	1929–11–7–9	1.56	12:00	Type 100 (AV 3b)
408	1915–1–8–80	1.57	12:00	Type 101 (AV 3c(i))
409	1910–12–7–1	1.60	12:00	Type 104 (AV 3d)
410	1989–5–18–340	1.58	11:00	Type 108 (AV 3h)

Kaleb
Gold

Type 110 (Kaleb AV 4; Munro-Hay 1984, p. 124; J-J 205)

Obv. As above, but with the legend: ✠ΧΑΛΗΒΒΑΕΙΛΕΥϹΙ✠ (King Kaleb).

On J-J 205 the last letter is clearer, and looks like Γ.

Rev. As Type 91, but no monogram, and the legend: ✠✠ΒΑϹΙΛΕΥϹ✠ (King). One example (Vaccaro 1967, 32) reads: ✠✠ΑΒϹΙΛΕΥϹ✠.

Kaleb
Silver

Type 111 (Kaleb AR 1; Munro-Hay 1984, p. 125)

Obv. Head and shoulders bust r., crowned. Cross at top. Ge'ez legend: ንጉሠ✠ከለበ (King Kaleb).
Rev. Head and shoulders bust r., wearing headcloth, Cross at top. Ge'ez legend: ለሀገረ✠ዘየደለ (He who is fitting for the city; or, May this please the country).

411	1969–6–24–9	0.66	12:00
412	1989–5–18–341	0.47	11:00

Kaleb
Bronze

Type 112 (Kaleb AE 1; Munro-Hay 1984, p. 126)

Obv. As Type 76 (Anonymous AE 2) obv., but with no extra cross behind head, and the legend: Χ Α ΛΗΒ (Khaleb).
Rev. As Type 76 (Anonymous AE 2). The legend appears to vary, beginning ΤΟΥΟΤ. . . or written retrograde and incorrectly: . . .ΧΗΤΗϹΑΛΥΟΥ. . .

413	1880–6–4–29	0.76

Types 113–114 (Kaleb AE 2–3; Munro-Hay 1984, p. 126). Both are unexamined pieces in the Aksum Museum. One of them may be of the Type 111i (J-J 382), a bronze version of Kaleb's silver Type 111.

The Later Christian Period, *c.* AD 540–640

Ella Amida (Allamidas/'Allamiruis')
Gold

Types 115–116 (Type 115, Alla Amidas AV 1, Munro-Hay 1984, p. 129. Type 116, Allamiruis AV 1, Munro-Hay 1984, p. 130; J-J 198)

Obv. Half-length bust r., crowned, flanked by two wheat-stalks, all enclosed in a beaded circle. Cross at top. Greek legend all round: ✠ΑΛΛΑΜΙΔΑC (Ella Amida) and variants. The 'Allamiruis' type (Type 116) reads: ✠ΑΛΛΑΜΙΡΥΙC, the letter P being on its side. This seems to be merely a deformed version of the legend rather than the name of a separate ruler.

Rev. Same as one die of Type 110 rev. (Kaleb AV 4): ✠✠ΑΒCΙΛΕΥC✠. The 'Allamiruis' type reads, from the top clockwise: ✠✠VΛCΙΛCΙWCΙ✠ which appears to be a degraded writing of 'Basileus'.

Za-yaʿabiyo la madhen negus/WZN (Wazena)
Silver

Type 117 (Za-yaʿabiyo la madhen negus, WZN (Wazena), AR 3; Munro-Hay 1984, p. 144. N.B. also Juel-Jensen 1987ii; J-J 175)

Obv. Head and shoulders bust, facing, crowned. The crown is often gilt, and on one variant within the main type (Type 117i) described by Juel-Jensen (1987ii) it is depicted as an arched diadem, gilded, with a small cross on it. There may be symbols in the field (dot, cross, crescent). Cross at top. Geʿez legend: ንጉሡ✠ወዘነ (King WZN – customarily vocalised as 'Wazena').

Rev. Arch supported by columns with bases and capitals in centre field, containing Greek-style cross with gold-inlaid punch-hole. Geʿez legend all round: ዘየዐበየለመደነ፥✠ነገሡ (The King who exalts the Saviour); or, perhaps (Godet 1986) it should be read as LMDHNT-NGS ZYʿBY, 'Le salut du roi, ceci (or: ce que) l'accroît', which takes the cross as a letter T, commencing the legend at the top of the coin.

Wazena
Bronze

Types 118–123 (Wazena AE 1; Munro-Hay 1984, pp. 140–41: Type 123; Tedesco-Zammarano 1947, 8)

Obv. Half-length bust r., wearing headcloth and holding a wheat-stalk topped sometimes with a cross, which breaks the legend at different places; there are many different varieties of arrangement. Sometimes a cross is inserted into the legend separately from the wheat-stalk. Symbols (a dot or group of dots, cross, crescent) may appear in the field. Geʿez legend: ለአሕዘበየደለ (He who is fitting for the people).

Type 118 reads LAHZBZY wheat-stalk DL
Type 119 reads LAHZ✠B wheat-stalk ZYDL
Type 120 reads LAHZBZ wheat-stalk sceptre cruciger YDL
Type 121 reads LAHZBZ wheat-stalk YDL
Type 122 reads LAHZBZY wheat-stalk DL
Type 123 reads LAHZBZ(very small +)Y wheat-stalk DL

Rev. Cross with four arms extending to the edges of the coin, where they terminate in smaller crosses dividing the legend. Punch-hole inlaid with gold in the centre of the cross, and four short intermediary arms terminating in hammer heads. Geʿez legend: ✠ዘወዘነ✠ነዘነገሡ (Of Wazena, of the King; or, Of the King Za-Wazen).

Die-axes vary

414	1969–6–24–22	1.48	Type 118	
415	1953–4–2–21	1.48	Type 119	
416	1953–4–2–23	0.48	Uncertain type	
417	1989–5–18–403	0.82	Type 118	
418	1989–5–18–404	1.56	Uncertain type	
419	1989–5–18–405	1.27	Type 118	
420	1989–5–18–406	1.40	Type 120	Three dots upper r. obv.
421	1989–5–18–407	0.95	Type 120	
422	1989–5–18–408	1.17	Type 121	Small cross upper r. obv.
423	1989–5–18–409	1.09	Type 120	
424	1989–5–18–410	0.59	Uncertain type	
425	1989–5–18–411	1.03	Type 121	
426	1989–5–18–412	1.28	Type 120	Crescent l. obv.
427	1989–5–18–413	1.03	Type 120	
428	1989–5–18–414	1.36	Type 120/121?	
429	1989–5–18–415	0.60	Type 120	Crescent upper r. obv.
430	1989–5–18–416	1.01	Type 118	Small cross upper r. obv.
431	1989–5–18–417	1.50	Type 119	
432	1989–5–18–418	1.07	Type 118?	
433	1989–5–18–419	1.10	Type 121	
434	1989–5–18–420	1.56	Type 121?	
435	1989–5–18–421	1.09	Type 118	Small cross upper r. obv.
436	1989–5–18–422	0.50	Type 121?	
437	1989–5–18–423	1.19	Type 121	Crescent upper r. obv.

Ella Gabaz
Gold

Type 124 (Ella Gabaz AV 1; Munro-Hay 1984, p. 131)

Obv. Half-length bust r., crowned, flanked by two wheat-
stalks, one of which the king is holding in his hand,
all enclosed in a beaded circle. Cross at top. Greek
legend all round: ✠ΛΛΛΑΓΑΒΑΖΝΓ (Neg[us?] Ella
Gabaz). The British Museum example has an Ɛ on its
side as the first letter.

Rev. As obv. but wearing headcloth. Greek legend all
round: ✠ΒΑ✠ΣΙ✠ΛƐ✠ΥϹ (King); some examples have
✠ΒΑ✠ΛΙ✠ΛƐ✠ΥϹ.

438 1929–11–7–10   1.75   12:00

Za-yaʿabiyo la madḫen negus/anonymous
Silver

Type 125 (Za-yaʿabiyo la madḫen negus, anonymous, AR 1;
Munro-Hay 1984, p. 142)

Obv. Head and shoulders bust, facing, crowned. The crown,
in which sometimes three vertical divisions can be
seen, is often gilt. There may be symbols on the field
(dot, cross). Cross at top. Geʿez legend: ነገሠ✠አከሰመ
(King of Aksum).

Type 125i (Juel-Jensen coll., J-J 393) has a variant legend
written NGSA✠KSM.
Type 125ii (Walburg 289) lacks the cross altogether.

Rev. Arch supported by columns with bases and capitals in
centre field, containing a square-armed cross voided
and inlaid with gold. Geʿez legend all round, with the
✠ and the word NGS usually below the arch:
ዘየዐበየለመደገነ✠ነገሠ (The King who exalts the
Saviour).

439 1989–5–18–424   1.09   11:00   Dot r. obv.

Za-yaʿabiyo la madḫen negus/AGD
Silver

Type 126 (Za-yaʿabiyo la madḫen negus, AGD, AR 2; Munro-
Hay 1984, p. 143)

Obv. As above but no cross at top, and the monogram 𝕬
(AGD) l. of head: ነገሠአከሳመ (AGD: King of
Aksum). The crown may be curved or sub-rectangular
outlined by dots. Vowelling is ocasionally present on
certain letters (N, G, S, M) on the obverse.

Rev. As Type 125 rev.

440 1969–6–24–21   1.05   12:00
441 1989–5–18–425   1.01   11:00
442 1989–5–18–426   1.03   12:00   Dot r. obv.; last
                                           letter of legend only
                                           under arch
443 1989–5–18–427   1.01   12:00
444 1989–5–18–428   0.95   11:00
445 1989–5–18–429   0.88   12:00

Ioel
Gold

Type 127 (Ioel AV 1; Munro-Hay 1984, p. 132)

Obv. Half-length bust to r., crowned, flanked by two
wheat-stalks. Greek legend: ✠ΒΑϹΙΛΕΥϹΑξWΜΙΤ
(King of the Aksumit[es]).

Rev. As obv. but wearing headcloth. Greek legend:
✠ΜϹΙΛƐΥϹΙWΗΛW (probably for ΙWΗΛ
Β✠ΑϹΙΛƐΥϹ, King Ioel).

Ioel
Gold

Type 128 (Ioel AV 2; Munro-Hay 1984, p. 133)

Obv. Half-length bust r., crowned, flanked by two wheat-
stalks, in a beaded circle; Greek legend all round:
ΒΑϹΙΛΙΑξWΜΙ (Kin[g] of (the) Aksumi[tes]).

Rev. As obv., but wearing headcloth: ✠Ι✠W✠Η✠Λ (Ioel).

446 1921–3–16–2   1.48   3:00

Ioel
Silver

Type 129 (Ioel AR 1; Munro-Hay 1984, p. 134)

Obv. Head and shoulders bust, facing, wearing cap (?) with
cross on front, and pendilia or ears shown at the sides.
Sometimes symbols in the field. Geʿez legend round
upper part of coin: ነገሠአየአል (King Ioel).

Rev. Very small Greek cross in circle. The centre has a
punch-hole inlaid with gold. Greek legend all round:
ΑΡΕϹΗΧΥ (By the grace of Ch[rist?]).

Die-axes vary
447 1968–4–1–6   0.99   Small crescent r. of head obv.
448 1989–5–18–342 0.68
449 1989–5–18–343 0.72   Dot r. of head obv.

Ioel
Silver

Type 130 (Ioel AR 2; Munro-Hay 1984, p. 135)

Obv. Head and shoulders bust r., crowned, dividing the
legend into two groups of letters. Sometimes symbol
(crescent) r. of head (not on British Museum
examples). Geʿez legend: አየ አለ (Ioel).

Rev. Half-length bust r., wearing headcloth, holding hand-
cross. The legend is divided by the king's head. Geʿez
legend: ነገ ሠ (King).

450 1969–6–24–18   1.04   7:00
451 1989–5–18–344   0.91   8:00

Ioel
Bronze
Types 131–132 (Ioel AE 1; Munro-Hay 1984, p. 136)

Obv. Head and shoulders bust r., crowned, with a cross in the centre top of the crown. Symbols may appear in the field. The king's head divides the legend. Geʿez legend beginning either near the top right (Type 131) or near the bottom left (Type 132) of the coin: **ንገ ሠ** (King).
Rev. Greek cross in centre field, sometimes with central boss, dividing Geʿez legend: **አ የ አ ለ** (Ioel).

Die-axes vary

452	1915–2–5–1	1.14	Type 131
453	1930–10–6–1	0.45	
454	1989–5–18–345	0.99	Small cross r. obv.
455	1989–5–18–346	1.24	
456	1989–5–18–348	0.46	Small cross r. obv.
457	1989–5–18–349	0.95	Small cross r. obv. Dot between the letters N and G of legend r.
458	1989–5–18–350	1.05	Small cross r. obv., three dots left
459	1989–5–18–351	0.76	Small cross r. obv., dot l.
460	1989–5–18–352	1.27	Small cross r. obv., bar l
461	1989–5–18–353	0.79	
462	1989–5–18–354	0.48	
463	1989–5–18–356	1.03	Small cross r. obv.
464	1989–5–18–359	0.86	
465	1989–5–18–360	0.81	Small cross r. obv.
466	1989–5–18–363	1.38	Small cross r. obv., crescent (?) l.
467	1989–5–18–364	0.81	
468	1989–5–18–366	0.90	Small cross r. obv.
469	1989–5–18–368	0.97	Small cross r. obv., dot l.
470	1989–5–18–370	1.57	Small cross r. obv., dot between letters N and G of legend
471	1953–4–2–1	0.73	Small cross r. obv. Type 132
472	1989–5–18–347	1.01	Small cross r. obv., dot l.
473	1989–5–18–355	1.12	Small cross r. obv., bar l?
474	1989–5–18–357	1.07	Small cross r. obv., dot l.
475	1989–5–18–358	0.41	Small cross r. obv.
476	1989–5–18–361	1.13	Small cross r. obv., bar l.
477	1989–5–18–362	0.92	Small cross r. obv.
478	1989–5–18–365	0.70	Small cross r., dot l.
479	1989–5–18–367	0.99	Small cross r. obv.
480	1989–5–18–369	1.19	Small cross r. obv., bar l.

Ioel
Bronze
Type 133 (Ioel AE 2; Munro-Hay 1984, p. 137)
Obv. and rev. as Type 129 (Ioel AR 1).

Ioel
Bronze
Type 134 (Ioel AE 3; Munro-Hay 1984, p. 138)

Obv. Head and shoulders bust, facing, crowned, with a cross in the centre top of the crown. Ears or pendilia on both sides, and symbols in the field. Geʿez legend: **ንገሠአየአለ** (King Ioel).
Rev. Latin cross in the centre field, sometimes with a central voided dot. Geʿez legend: **ክረሰተሰመሰለን** (Christ is with us), always written **ክረሰተሰመአለን**.

Die-axes very variable

481	1969–6–24–19	1.19	
482	1969–6–24–20	0.95	Small cross r. obv.
483	1989–5–18–371	0.68	
484	1989–5–18–372	0.69	Small dot r. obv.
485	1989–5–18–373	0.84	
486	1989–5–18–374	0.84	
487	1989–5–18–375	0.65	Three dots r. obv.
488	1989–5–18–376	0.65	Three (?) dots r. obv.
489	1989–5–18–377	0.72	Dot r. obv.
490	1989–5–18–378	1.01	Three dots r. obv.
491	1989–5–18–379	0.84	Small crescent (?) r. obv.
492	1989–5–18–380	0.75	Three dots r. obv.
493	1989–5–18–381	1.02	
494	1989–5–18–382	0.81	
495	1989–5–18–383	0.76	
496	1989–5–18–384	0.78	
497	1989–5–18–385	0.56	
498	1989–5–18–386	0.96	
499	1989–5–18–387	0.43	
500	1989–5–18–388	1.15	
501	1989–5–18–389	0.77	Small crescent (?) r. obv.
502	1989–5–18–390	0.88	
503	1989–5–18–391	0.84	
504	1989–5–18–392	0.65	Dot r. obv.
505	1989–5–18–393	1.01	Small cross r. obv.
506	1989–5–18–394	1.17	
507	1989–5–18–395	0.68	Dot r. obv.
508	1989–5–18–396	0.71	Three dots l. obv.
509	1989–5–18–397	0.56	
510	1989–5–18–398	0.63	Small crescent (?) r. obv.
511	1989–5–18–399	0.99	Dot r. obv.
512	1989–5–18–400	1.02	
513	1989–5–18–401	1.06	Three dots r. obv.?
514	1989–5–18–402	1.04	Dot r. obv.

Ioel
Bronze
Type 135 (Ioel AE 4; Munro-Hay 1984, p. 139)
Obv. and rev. as Type 130 (Ioel AR 2).

Ḥataz ('Iathlia')
Gold
Type 136 (Iathlia AV 1; Munro-Hay 1984, p. 151)

Obv. Half-length bust r., crowned, flanked by two wheat-stalks, one of which he is holding in his hand, all in beaded circle. Greek legend: BACIΛIAξWMI (Kin[g] of (the) Aksum[ites]).

Rev. As obv. but wearing headcloth. Greek legend: ⳩IA⳨ΘⳋΛIⳋA ('Iathlia' = Iathaza(?) = Ḥataz?).

Ḥataz
Silver
Type 137 (Ḥataz AR 1; Munro-Hay 1984, p. 157)

Obv. Half-length bust, facing, holding hand-cross in front of chest. There are pendilia on either side of the crown. There may be symbols (dots, cross) in the field. The king's head divides the legend. Ge'ez legend: ነገሠ ሐተዘ (King Ḥataz).

Rev. Central cross contained in diamond terminating at the corners four crosses breaking the legend. Ge'ez legend: ሠⳋሀለⳋለአⳋሐዘⳋበ (Mercy to the people).

Die-axes vary
515	1989–5–18–498	0.81
516	1989–5–18–499	0.67
517	1989–5–18–500	0.88 Dot l. obv.

Ḥataz
Silver
Types 138–139 (Ḥataz AR 2a, AR 2b; Munro-Hay 1984, pp. 158–9)

Obv. Head and shoulders bust r., crowned, dividing the legend. Ge'ez legend: ሐ ተዣ (Ḥataz).

Rev. Half-length bust r., wearing headcloth, holding hand-cross. The king's head divides the legend. Ge'ez legend: ነገ ሠ (King).

The only difference between Types 138 and 139 (AR 2a and 2b) is that the obv. legend of Type 139 (AR 2b) commences at right instead of left side.

Ḥataz
Bronze
Type 140 (Ḥataz AE 1; Munro-Hay 1984, p. 160)

Obv. Head and shoulders bust, facing, crowned. There are pendilia (or ears?) represented at the sides, and a small cross surmounts the crown at top. The bust is flanked by two wheat-stalks, from the base of which spring two stems topped with crosses which flank the king's shoulders.

Rev. Central Greek cross in octagonal frame. Ge'ez legend all round: ሐተዘነገሠአክሰም (Ḥataz King of Aksum).

Die-axes vary
518	1969–6–24–24	0.91
519	1989–5–18–501	1.13
520	1989–5–18–502	0.80
521	1989–5–18–503	0.94
522	1989–5–18–504	1.71
523	1989–5–18–505	0.78
524	1989–5–18–506	0.81
525	1989–5–18–507	1.47
526	1989–5–18–508	0.34
527	1989–5–18–509	0.34
528	1989–5–18–528	0.93

Ḥataz
Bronze
Type 141 (Ḥataz AE 2; Munro-Hay 1984, p. 161)

Obv. As Type 137 (Ḥataz AR 1).
Rev. As Type 137 (Ḥataz AR 1). The central cross often has tripartite ends to its arms.

Die-axes vary
529	1925–9–2–2	0.69
530	1953–4–2–2	0.88
531	1953–4–2–3	0.24
532	1953–4–2–4	0.74
533	1953–4–2–5	0.93
534	1953–4–2–6	1.05
535	1989–5–18–510	0.63
536	1989–5–18–511	0.99
537	1989–5–18–512	0.99
538	1989–5–18–513	0.80
539	1989–5–18–514	0.69
540	1989–5–18–515	0.82
541	1989–5–18–516	0.65
542	1989–5–18–517	0.37
543	1989–5–18–518	0.88
544	1989–5–18–519	0.70
545	1989–5–18–520	0.37
546	1989–5–18–521	0.49
547	1989–5–18–522	0.60
548	1989–5–18–523	0.78
549	1989–5–18–524	0.67
550	1989–5–18–525	0.51
551	1989–5–18–526	0.73
552	1989–5–18–527	0.52
553	1989–5–18–529	0.91

Ḥataz
Bronze
Type 142 (Ḥataz AE 3; Munro-Hay 1984, p. 162)
Obv. and rev as Type 138 (Ḥataz AR 2a).

Israel
Gold
Type 143 (Israel AV 1; Munro-Hay 1984, p. 149; J-J 6, 147)

Obv. Half-length bust r., crowned, flanked by two wheat-stalks, one of which he is holding in his hand, all in beaded circle. Cross at top. Greek legend: ✠BACIΛIAξWMI (Kin[g] of (the) Aksumi[tes]).

Rev. As obv. but wearing headcloth: ✠IC✠PA✠H✠Λ (Israel).

Israel
Bronze
Type 144 (Israel AE 1; Munro-Hay 1984, p. 150)

Obv. Half-length bust r., crowned, holding hand-cross. Ge'ez legend: ንገሠየስረአለ (King Israel).

Rev. Central cross with flared arms, enclosed by a circle/diamond of dots. Ge'ez legend all round: ኡለአሐዘበሠበለⵕ (Peace to the people?). The first letter may stand for a cross.

554	1969–6–24–17	0.72	An extremely worn example

Gersem
Gold
Type 145 (Gersem AV 1; Munro-Hay 1984, p. 152)

Obv. Half-length bust, facing, holding cross l., with wheat-stalk r., all in beaded circle. Greek legend all round: ✠[BA]CIΛIAξWMI (Kin[g] of (the) Aksumi[tes]).

Rev. As Type 143 (Israel AV 1) rev., but with legend: ✠Γℰ✠PC✠ℰ✠M (Gersem).

Gersem
Gold
Type 146 (Gersem AV 2; Munro-Hay 1984, p. 153; J-J 201)

Obv. As Type 143 (Israel AV 1) obv., but with legend: ✠BACIΛIAξWMI (Kin[g] of (the) Aksumi[tes]).

Rev. Rudimentary half-length bust r., flanked by two wheat-stalks, one held in the hand. Greek legend all round: ✠Γℰ✠PC✠ℰ✠M (Gersem).

Gersem
Silver
Type 147 (Gersem AR 1; Munro-Hay 1984, p. 154)

Obv. Half-length bust r., crowned, holding hand-cross. There may be symbols in the field (dot, disc and crescent). The king's head divides the legend into two groups of letters. Ge'ez legend: ገረ ሰመ (Gersem).

Rev. As obv. but wearing headcloth. The Ge'ez legend may have vocalised letters: ንገ ሠ (King).

555	1969–6–24–23	0.61	9:00	Dot l. and disc and crescent r. obv.
556	1989–5–18–491	0.52	3:00	Dot l. obv; disc and crescent r. rev.
557	1989–5–18–492	1.20	6:00	Dot l. obv.
558	1989–5–18–493	0.48	3:00	
559	1989–5–18–494	0.08	10:00	Dot l. obv.; disc and crescent r. rev.

Gersem
Bronze
Types 148–149 (Gersem AE 1, 1a; Munro-Hay 1984, p. 155)

Obv. Half-length bust, facing, crowned, flanked by two crosses, one held in the hand. The crown has pendilia either side. The king's head divides the legend. Ge'ez legend: ንገሠ ገረሰመ (King Gersem). Type 149 (AE 1a) has a slight difference in the arrangement of the two parts of the legend: ንገሠገ ረሰመ.

Rev. Central cross enclosed in a diamond of dots, with larger dots at each point, and a cross (the T of Kristos in the legend) closing it at the top. Ge'ez legend all round: በክረስተሰመወአ (He conquers through Christ).

Die-axes vary widely

560	1953–4–2–22	1.08
561	1953–10–4–1	1.43
562	1970–4–20–1	0.91
563	1989–5–18–495	1.69
564	1989–5–18–496	1.97
565	1989–5–18–497	0.58

Gersem
Bronze
Type 150 (Gersem AE 2; Munro-Hay 1984, p. 156)
Obv. and rev. as Type 147 (Gersem AR 1).

Armaḥ
Silver
Type 151 (Armaḥ AR 1; Munro-Hay 1984, p. 145)

Obv. Half-length bust r., crowned, holding a hand-cross. Behind, l. a sceptre-cruciger consisting of a wheat-stalk topped with a cross. There may be various symbols in the field (dots, cross, disc and crescent). Ge'ez legend: ንገሠአረመሐ (King Armaḥ).

Rev. Pair of columns supporting an arch topped by a central Greek-style cross, voided and inlaid with gold, flanked by two smaller crosses on staves emerging from the capitals of the columns. Inside the arch, a key-shaped design consisting of a long triangle with a circle at the pointed end, also inlaid with gold. Ge'ez legend all round: ሠሀለመሰለመ (Mercy and peace).

566	1989–5–18–430	1.10	1:00	
567	1989–5–18–431	0.82	12:00	Small cross l. obv.
568	1989–5–18–432	0.99	12:00	Dot r. obv.
569	1989–5–18–433	0.80	12:00	Disc and crescent l. obv.
570	1989–5–18–434	0.79	12:00	Small crescent (?) l. obv.

Armaḥ

Bronze

Types 152–153 (Armaḥ AE 1, 1a; Munro-Hay 1984, pp. 147–8)

Obv. Full-length figure seated on high-backed chair, crowned and holding a long staff topped with a cross. There are many variants of style for both the figure and the chair. There may be small symbols in the field (dots, crescent etc). The royal figure divides the legend. Geʿez legend: ንገሥ ረምሐ (King Armaḥ).

Rev. Cross supported on a stem descending to a ring at the base of the coin, flanked by two wheat-stalks emerging from the same stem. The cross has a punch-hole in the centre, filled with gold.

Geʿez legend of the very rare Type 152 (AE 1): ፈሥሐወበሰለመለአሐዘበ (Joy and peace to the people); much commoner is Type 153 (AE 1a): ፈሥሐለየከነ ለአሐዘበ (Let there be joy to the people). The letter ፈ is sometimes reversed.

Die-axes vary widely

571	1953–4–2–8	1.71	Small cross behind head obv. Type 153
572	1869–1–1–1	2.60	Small cross behind head obv.
573	1989–5–18–435	1.72	Dot r. obv.
574	1989–5–18–436	2.02	Crescent behind head obv.
575	1989–5–18–437	2.12	Dot behind head l. obv. Pierced
576	1989–5–18–438	3.54	Small cross r. obv.
577	1989–5–18–439	1.66	
578	1989–5–18–440	1.20	
579	1989–5–18–441	1.48	Dot (?) r. obv.
580	1989–5–18–442	1.43	
581	1989–5–18–443	2.37	Small cross r. obv.
582	1989–5–18–444	1.37	Dot r. obv.
583	1989–5–18–445	2.38	Three dots bottom l. obv.
584	1989–5–18–446	1.67	Crescent l. obv.
585	1989–5–18–447	2.89	Dot r. obv.
586	1989–5–18–448	1.94	Small cross l. obv.
587	1989–5–18–449	2.25	Dot r. obv.
588	1989–5–18–450	1.35	
589	1989–5–18–451	1.45	Three dots r. obv.
590	1989–5–18–452	2.59	
591	1989–5–18–453	1.33	Triangle l. obv.
592	1989–5–18–454	2.01	
593	1989–5–18–455	1.31	Crescent r. obv.
594	1989–5–18–456	2.02	Small cross l. obv.

595	1989–5–18–457	1.36	
596	1989–5–18–458	1.65	
597	1989–5–18–459	2.59	
598	1989–5–18–460	1.73	
599	1989–5–18–461	2.23	Crescent r. obv.
600	1989–5–18–462	2.31	
601	1989–5–18–463	1.28	
602	1989–5–18–464	1.46	
603	1989–5–18–465	1.54	Dot r. obv.
604	1989–5–18–466	1.90	
605	1989–5–18–467	2.23	Dot r. obv.
606	1989–5–18–468	1.75	
607	1989–5–18–469	2.04	
608	1989–5–18–470	1.63	Small cross r. obv.
609	1989–5–18–471	1.50	Triangle l. obv.
610	1989–5–18–472	2.02	
611	1989–5–18–473	1.44	Dot l. obv.
612	1989–5–18–474	1.96	Crescent l. obv.
613	1989–5–18–475	1.23	
614	1989–5–18–476	1.81	
615	1989–5–18–477	1.49	
616	1989–5–18–478	2.48	Crescent l. obv.
617	1989–5–18–479	2.45	
618	1989–5–18–480	1.30	
619	1989–5–18–481	2.93	
620	1989–5–18–482	2.72	
621	1989–5–18–483	1.27	Γ (?) l. obv.
622	1989–5–18–484	2.35	
623	1989–5–18–485	1.29	Dot l. obv.
624	1989–5–18–486	1.39	
625	1989–5–18–487	2.30	
626	1989–5–18–488	1.79	Triangle (?) r. obv.
627	1989–5–18–489	2.26	Three dots l. obv.
628	1989–5–18–490	2.11	

Forgeries

Endubis. Type 1 (Endubis AV 1)

a   1989–5–18–530   3.14

Endubis. Type 2 (Endubis AR 1)

b   1989–5–18–531   2.13
c   1989–5–18–532   2.06
d   1989–5–18–533   2.13
e   1989–5–18–534   2.06
f   1989–5–18–535   2.54
g   1989–5–18–536   1.90
h   1989–5–18–537   2.27
i   1989–5–18–538   2.05
j   1989–5–18–539   2.03
k   1989–5–18–540   2.03

Aphilas. Type 8 (Aphilas AV 1)

l   1989–5–18–541   0.52

Aphilas. Type 9 (Aphilas AR 1)

m   1989–5–18–542   2.26

Ousanas. Type 26 (Ousanas AR 2)

n   1976–10–16–3   2.26
o   1989–5–18–543   2.06
p   1989–5–18–544   2.00

Ousana. Type 33 (Ousana without religious symbol AR 1)

q   1989–5–18–545   1.77
r   1989–5–18–546   1.54
s   1989–5–18–548   1.38

Ezanas. Type 41 (Ezanas pagan AE 2)

t   1989–5–18–549   1.82
u   1989–5–18–550   1.48

Ezanas. Type 42 (Ezanas without religious symbol AR 1, or
possibly Type 43, AR 1a?)

v   1989–5–18–547   1.23

Nezool. Type 82 (Nezool AV 1)

w   1989–5–18–551   2.31
x   1989–5–18–552   2.81

Plates

*All coins are reproduced
at twice actual size*

PLATE 1

1

2

3

4

5

6

7

8

9

Endubis

PLATE 2

10

11

12

13

14

15

16

17

18

19

20

21

Aphilas (10–20), Wazeba (21)

PLATE 3

22 23 24 25

26 27 28 29

30 31 32 33

Wazeba (22–5), Ousanas (25–33)

PLATE 4

34

35

36

37

38

39

40

41

42

43

44

45

Ousanas

PLATE 5

46   47   48   49

50   51   53

52

54   55   56   57

Ousanas (46–51), Ezanas (52–7)

PLATE 6

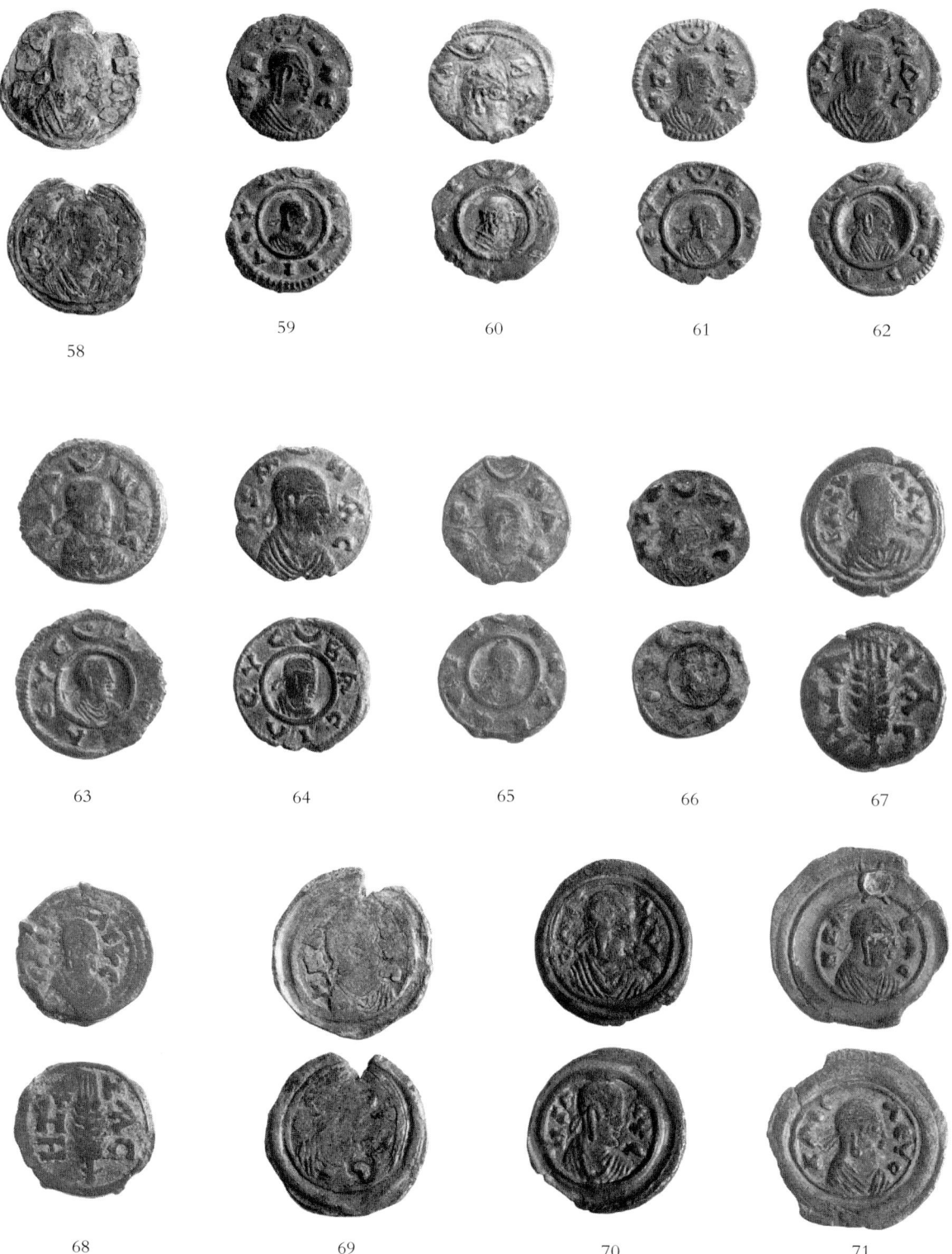

58

59

60

61

62

63

64

65

66

67

68

69

70

71

Ezanas

PLATE 7

72   73   74

75   76   77   78

79   80   81   82

Ezanas (72–5), Anonymous (76–82)

PLATE 8

83   84   85   86   87

88   89   90   91   92

95

93   94   96

Anonymous

PLATE 9

97

98

99

100

101

102

103

104

105

106

107

108

Anonymous

PLATE 10

109

110

111

112

113

114

115

116

117

118

119

120

Anonymous

PLATE 11

121   122   123   124

125   126   127   128

129   130   131   132

Anonymous

PLATE 12

133

134

135

136

137

138

139

140

141

142

Anonymous

PLATE 13

143

144

145

146

147

148

149

150

151

152

153

Anonymous

PLATE 14

154

155

156

157

158

159

160

161

162

163

164

165

Anonymous

PLATE 15

166

167

168

169

170

171

172

173

174

175

176

177

Anonymous

PLATE 16

178

179

180

181

182

183

184

185

186

187

188

Anonymous

PLATE 17

189

190

191

192

193

194

195

196

197

197a

198

199

Anonymous

PLATE 18

200   201   202   203

204   205   206   207

208   209   210   211

Anonymous

PLATE 19

212

213

214

215

216

217

218

219

220

221

222

223

Anonymous

PLATE 20

224

225

226

227

228

229

230

231

232

233

234

235

Anonymous

PLATE 21

236

237

238

239

240

241

242

243

244

Anonymous

PLATE 22

245

246

247

248

249

250

251

252

Ouazebas

PLATE 23

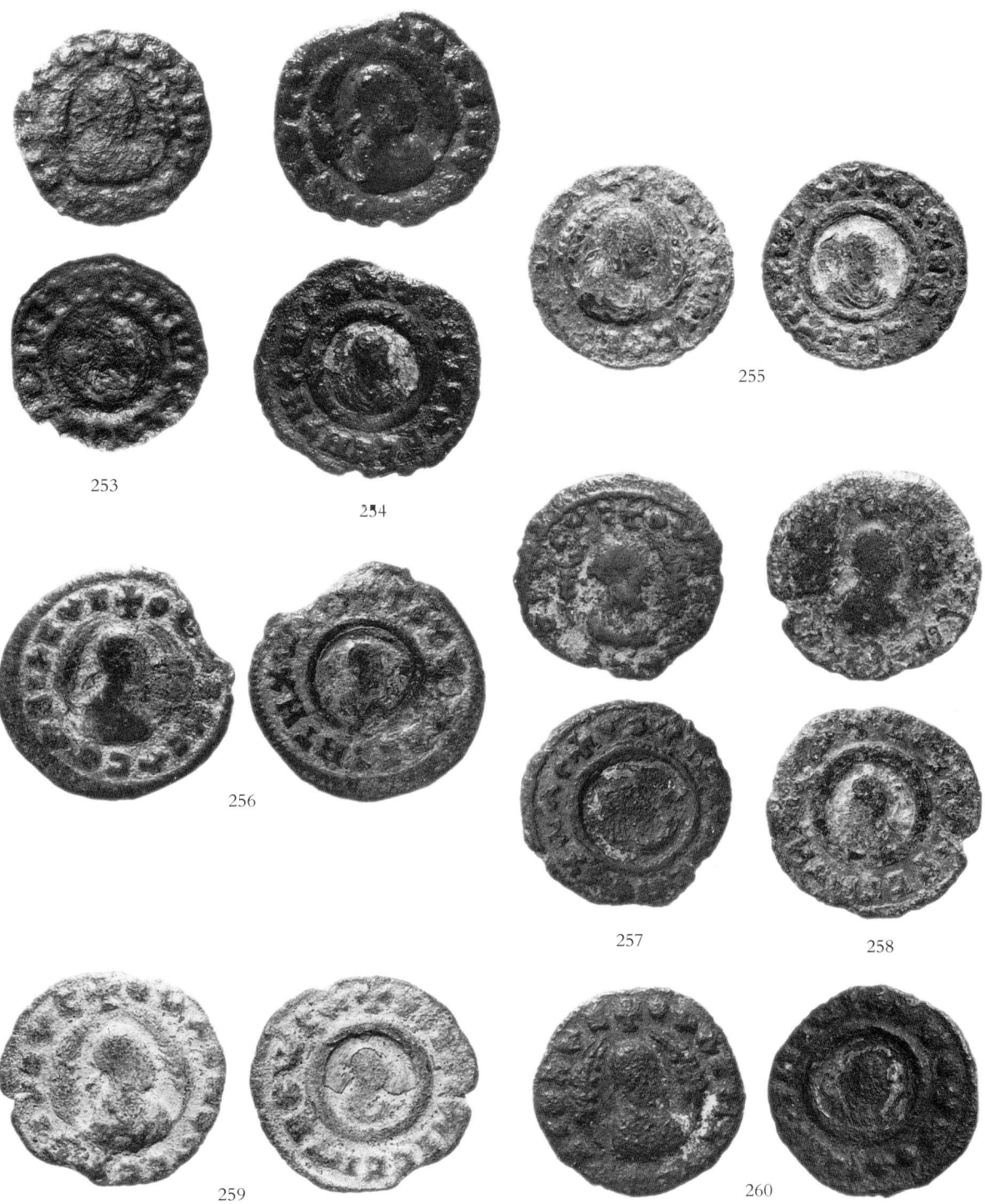

253

254

255

256

257

258

259

260

Ouazebas

PLATE 24

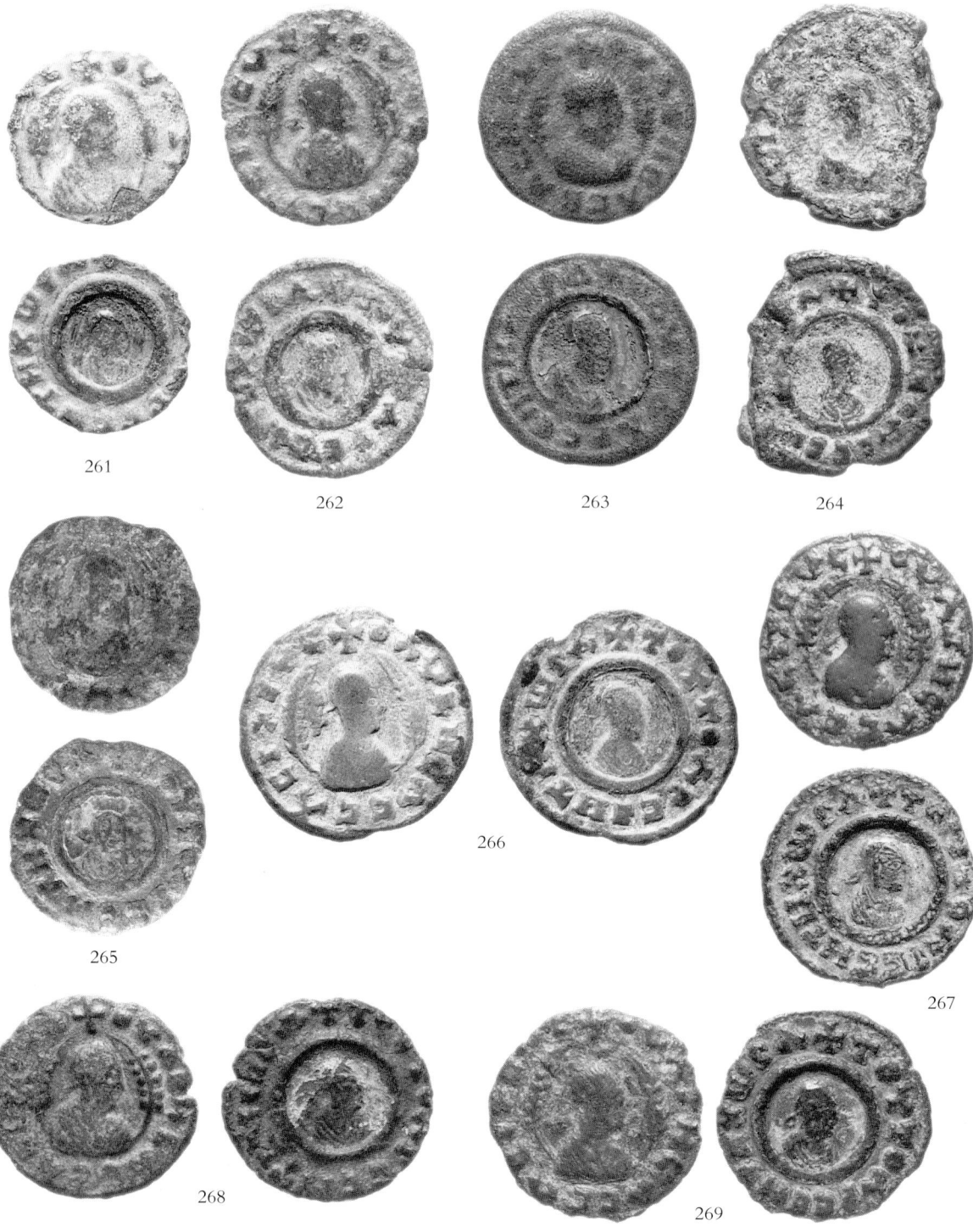

261

262

263

264

265

266

267

268

269

Ouazebas

PLATE 25

270

271

272

273

274

275

276

277

278

Ouazebas

PLATE 26

279

280

281

282

283

284

285

286

287

Ouazebas

PLATE 27

288

289

290

291

292

293

294

295

296

Ouazebas (288–9), Eon (290–91), Anonymous (292), Mḥḍys (293–6)

PLATE 28

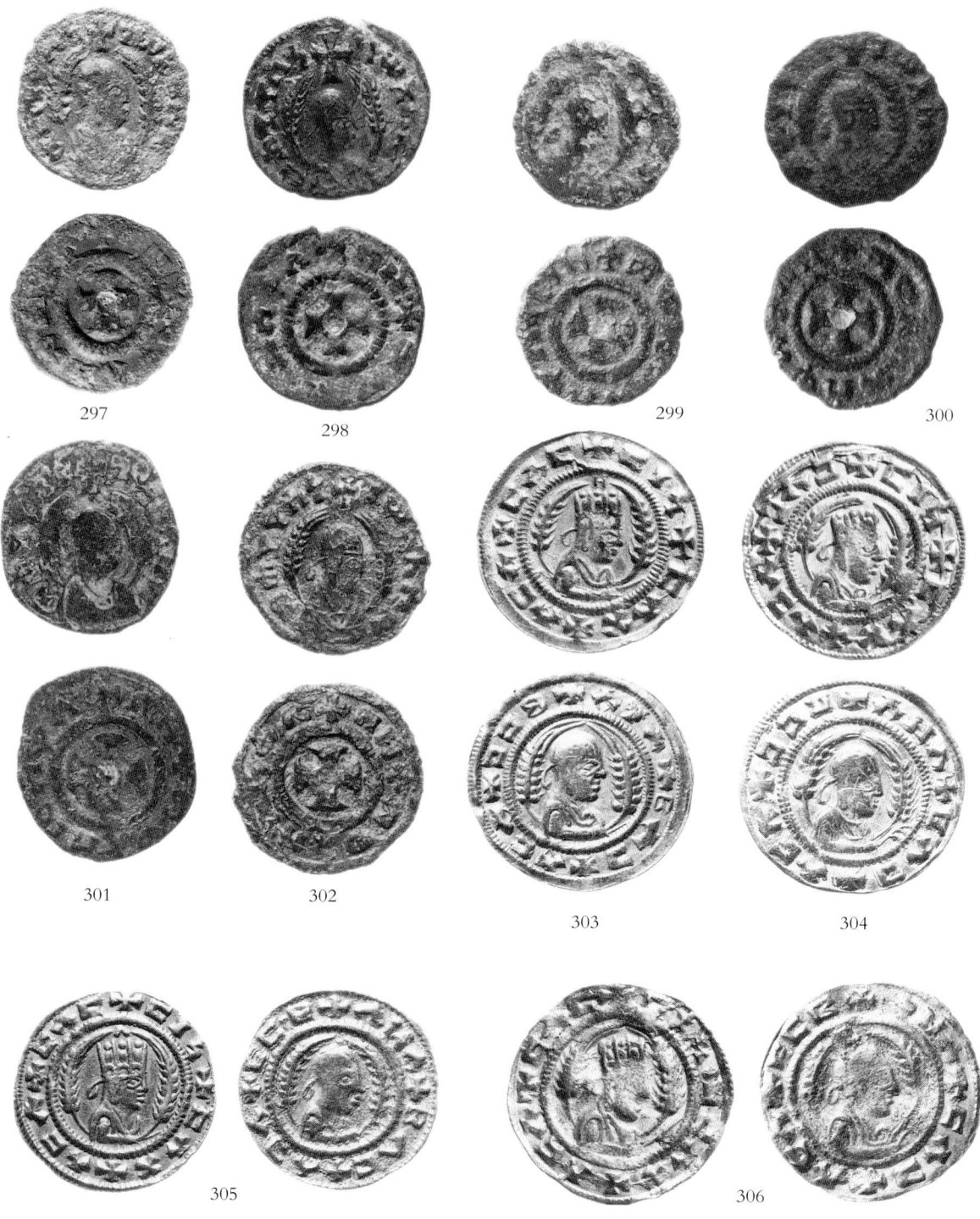

297   298   299   300

301   302   303   304

305   306

MHDYS (297–302), Ebana (303–6)

PLATE 29

307

308

309

310

311

312

313

314

315

316

Ebana (307–15), Anonymous (316)

PLATE 30

317

318

319

320

321

322

323

324

325

326

327

328

Anonymous

PLATE 31

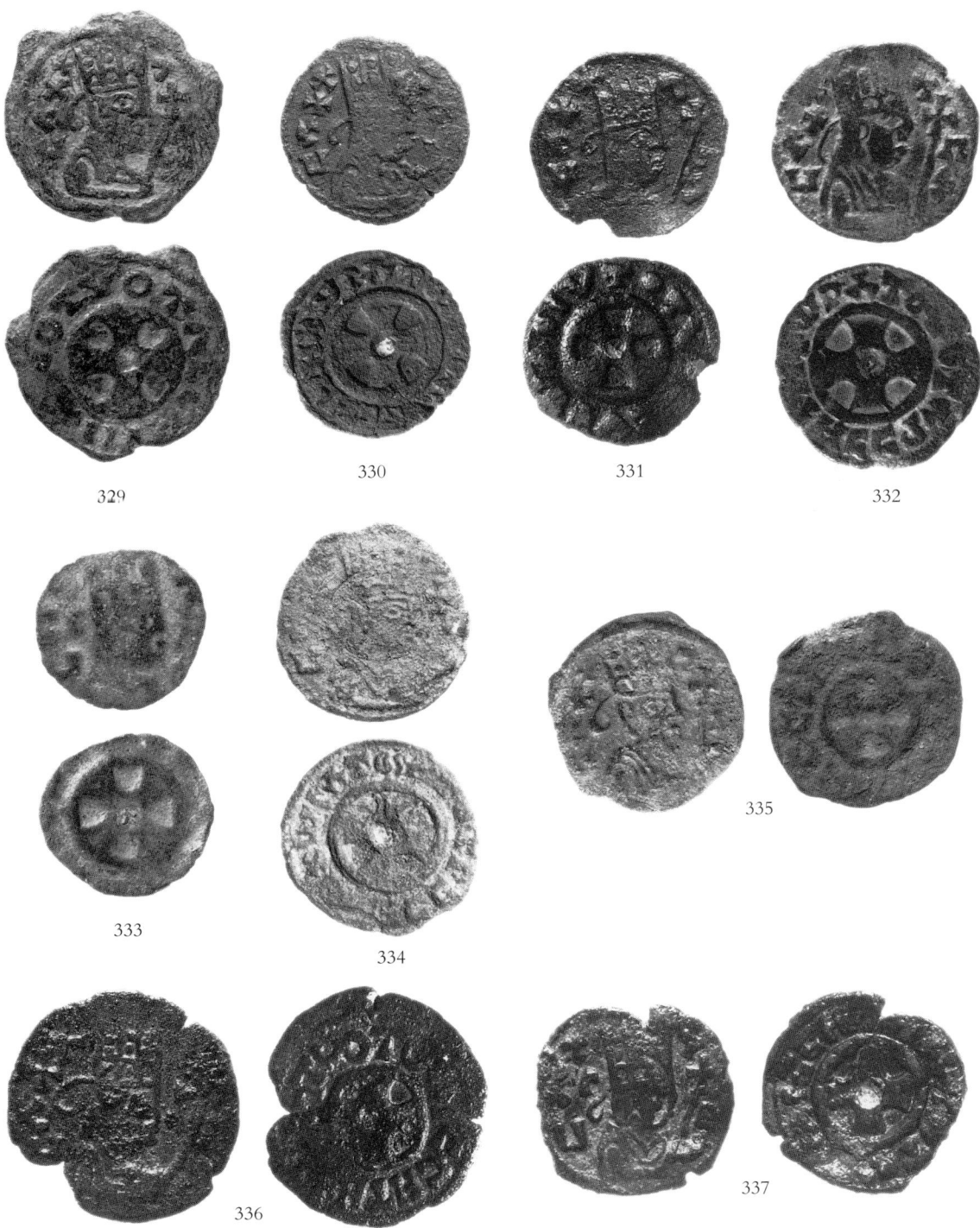

329

330

331

332

333

334

335

336

337

Anonymous

PLATE 32

338

339

340

341

342

343

344

345

346

347

Anonymous

PLATE 33

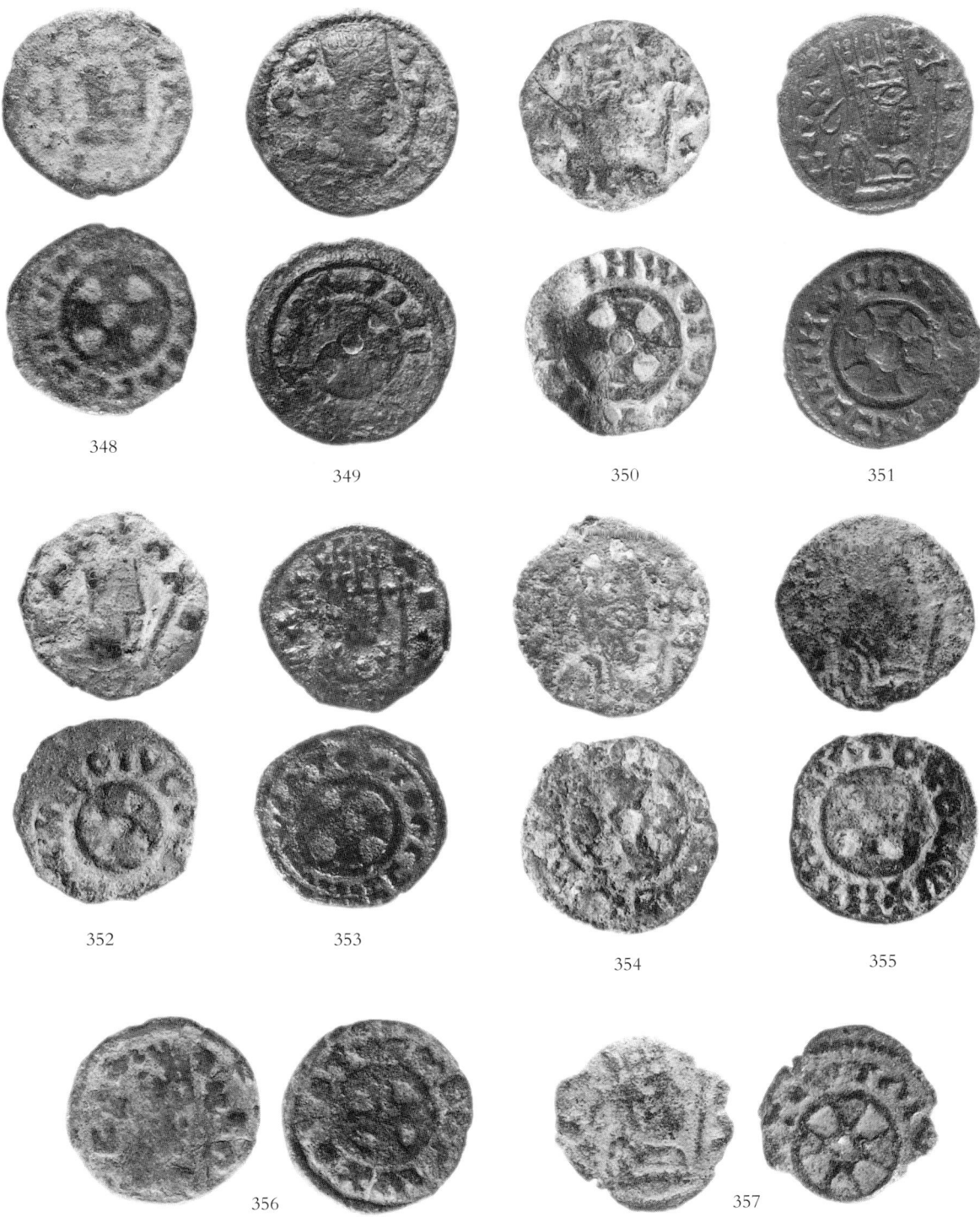

348

349

350

351

352

353

354

355

356

357

Anonymous

PLATE 34

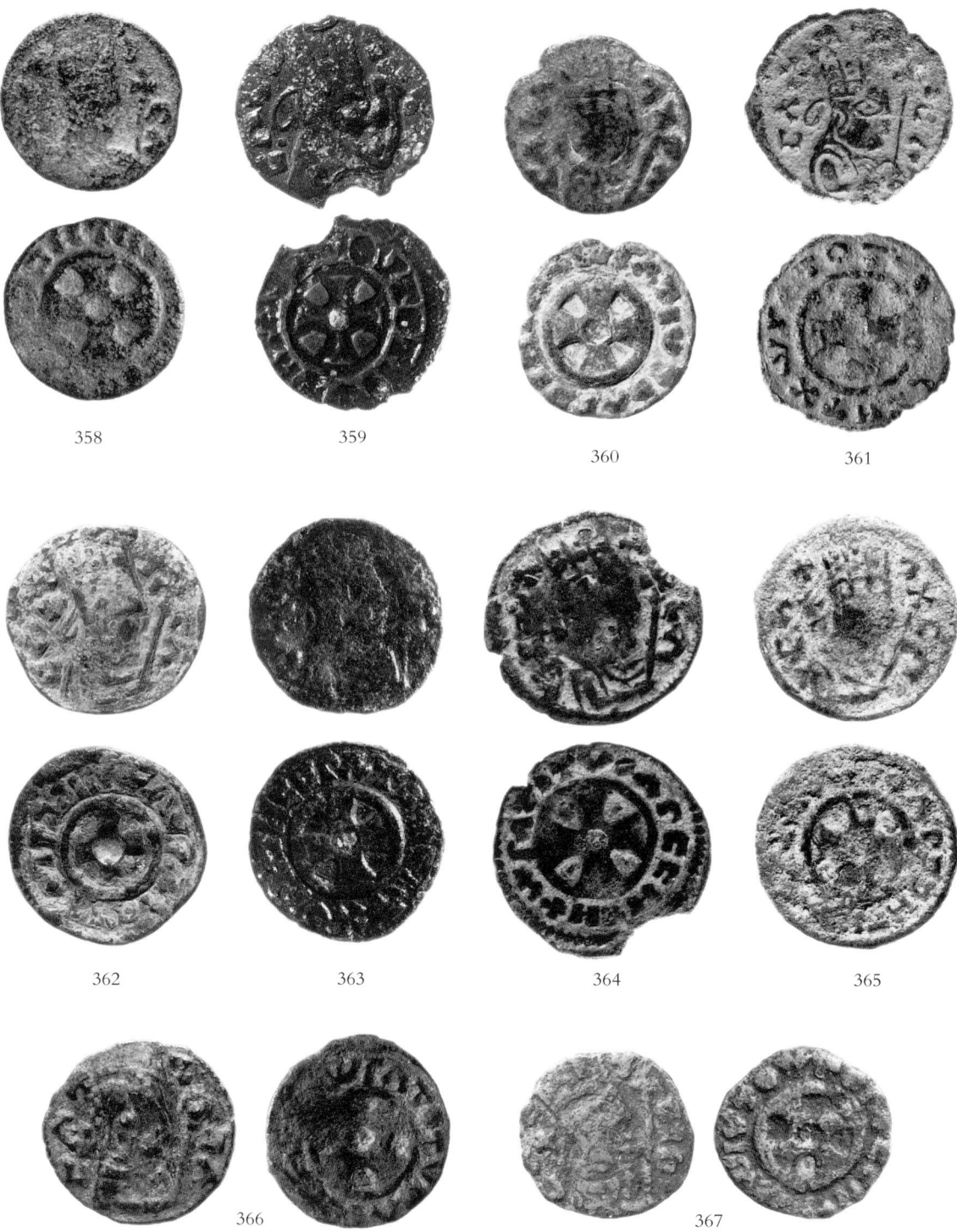

358

359

360

361

362

363

364

365

366

367

Anonymous

PLATE 35

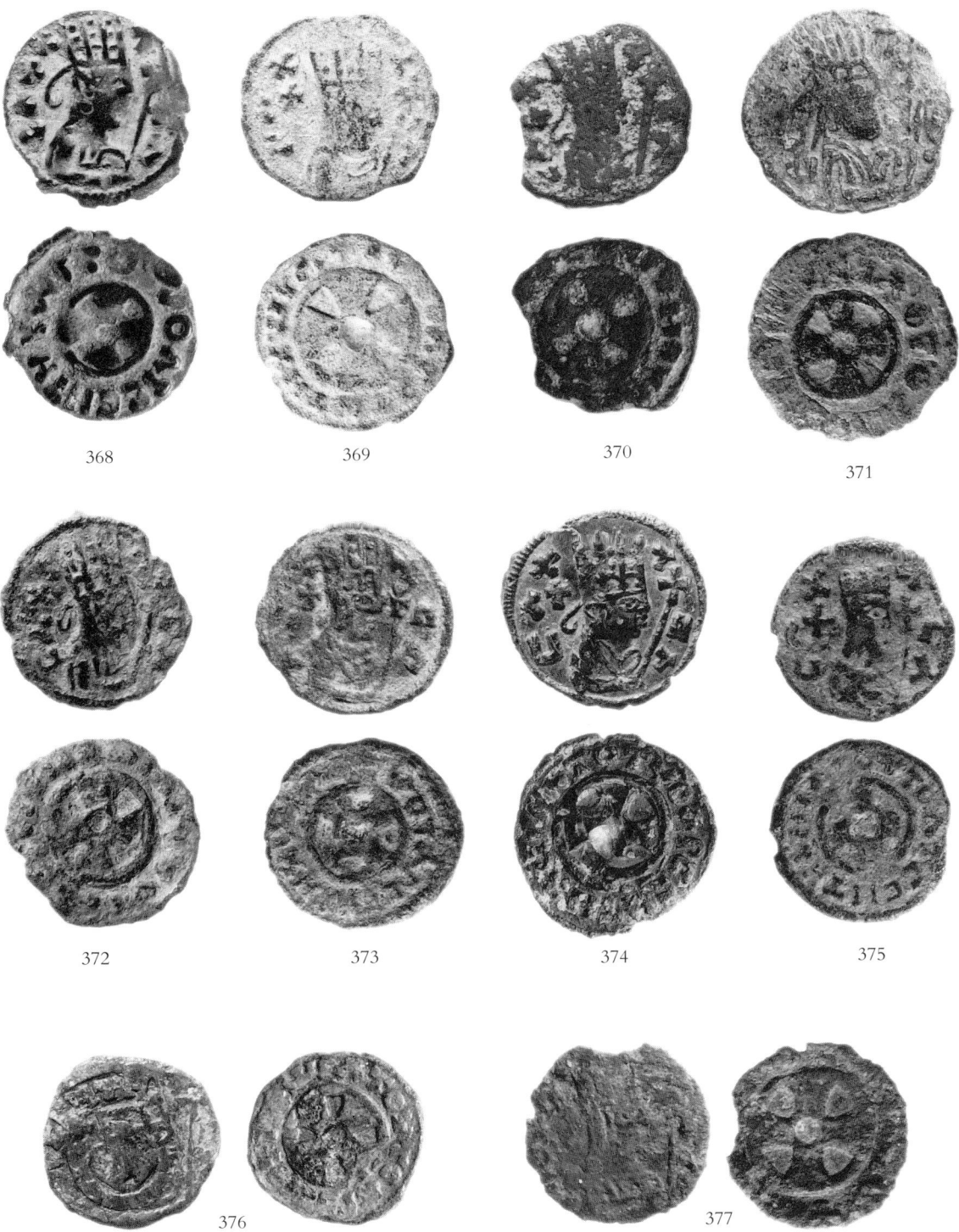

368

369

370

371

372

373

374

375

376

377

Anonymous

PLATE 36

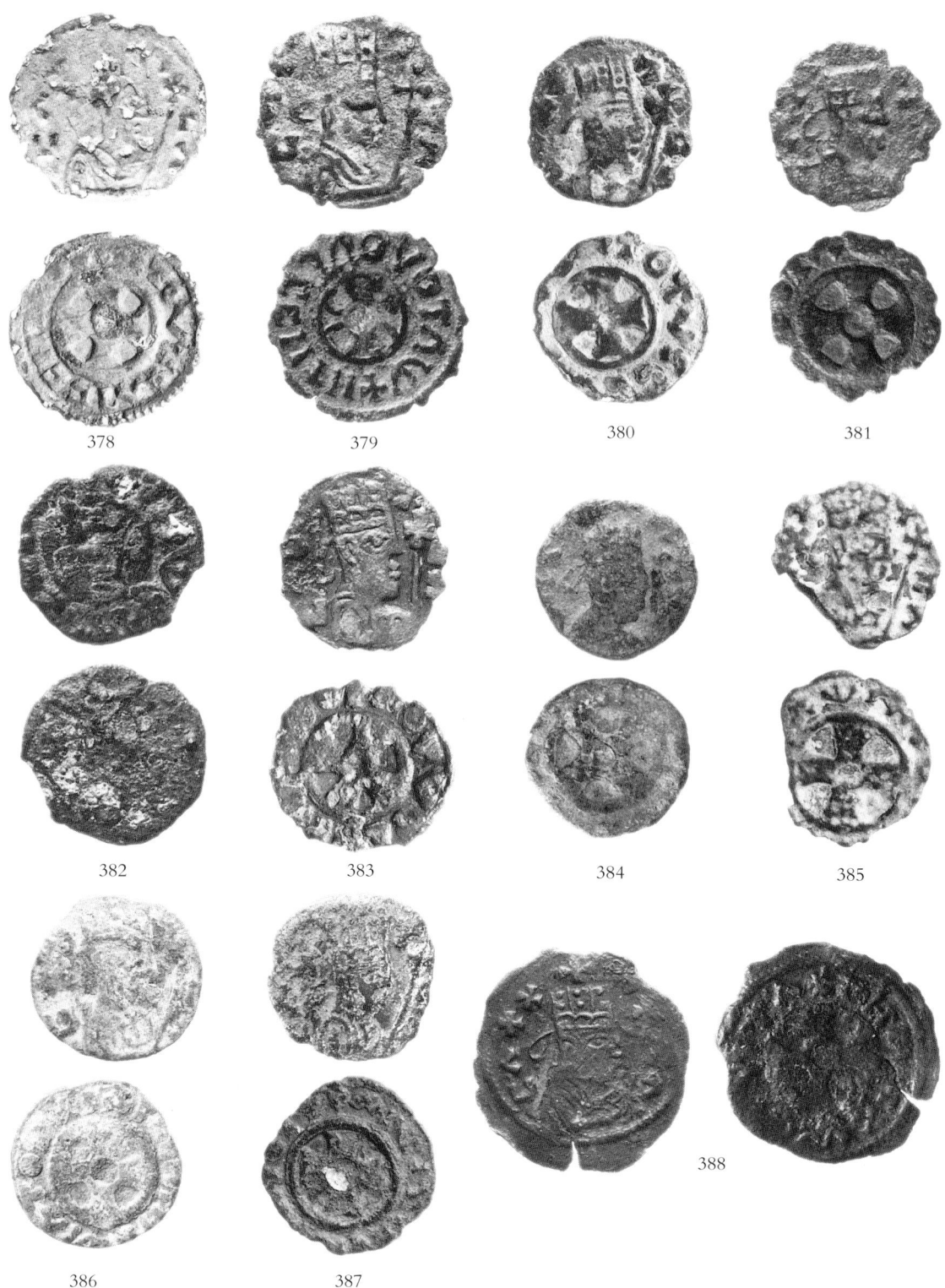

378

379

380

381

382

383

384

385

386

387

388

Anonymous

PLATE 37

389

390

391

392

393

394

395

396

397

398

399

Anonymous (389–98), Nezana (399)

PLATE 38

400

401

402

403

404

405

406

407

408

Nezana (400), Nezool (401), Ousas (402), Ousanas (403–5), Kaleb (406–8)

PLATE 39

409 410 411 412

413 414 415 416

417 418

Kaleb (409–13), Wazena (414–18)

PLATE 40

419

420

421

422

423

424

425

426

427

Wazena

PLATE 41

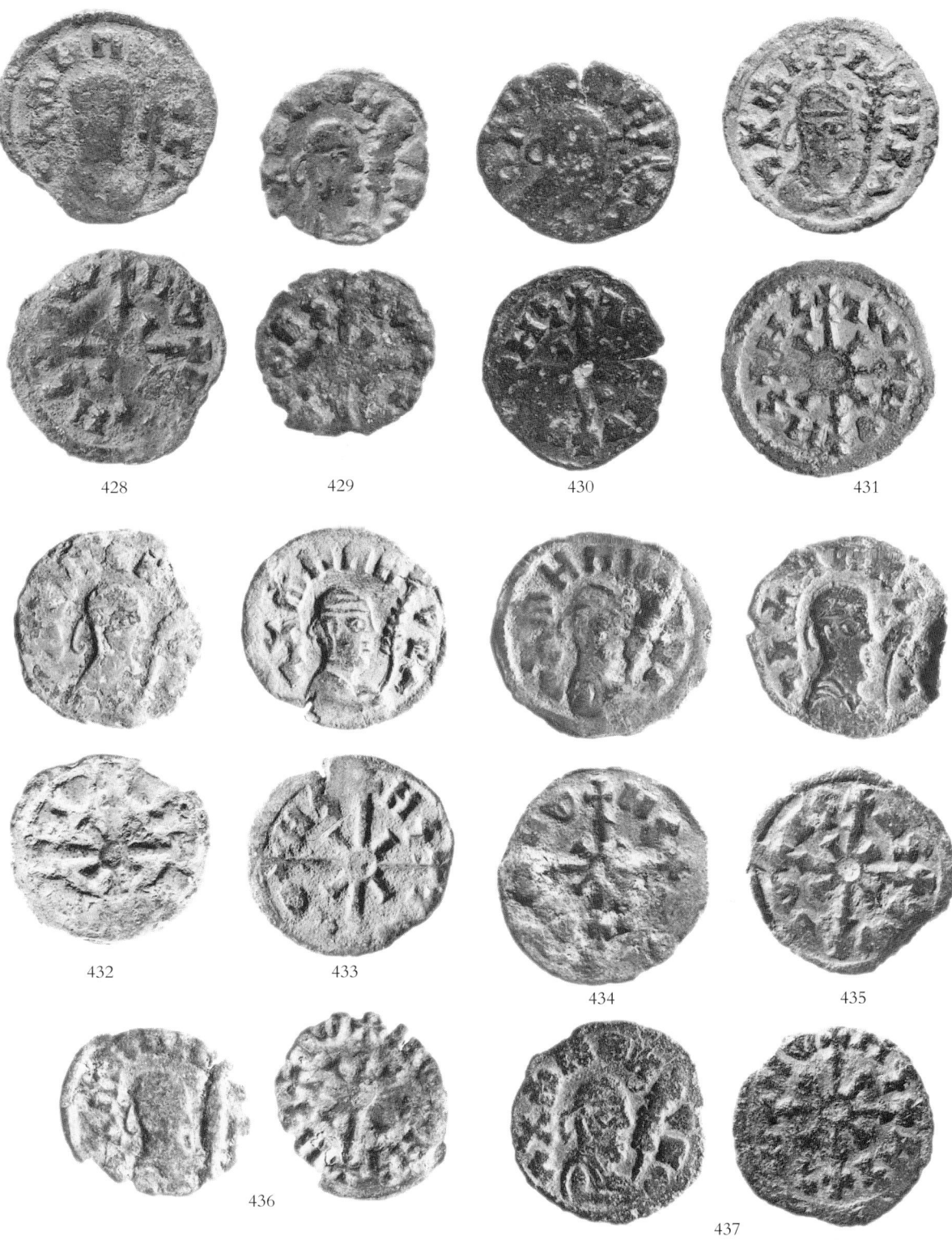

428   429   430   431

432   433

434   435

436

437

Wazena

PLATE 42

438 439 440 441

442 443 444

445

446 447

Ella Gabaz (438), Za-ya'abiyo la mad<u>h</u>en negus (439–45), Ioel (446–7)

PLATE 43

448   449

450   451

452   453   454   455

456   457   458   459

Ioel

PLATE 44

460

461

462

463

464

465

466

467

468

469

470

471

Ioel

PLATE 45

472

473

474

475

476

477

478

479

480

481

482

483

Ioel

PLATE 46

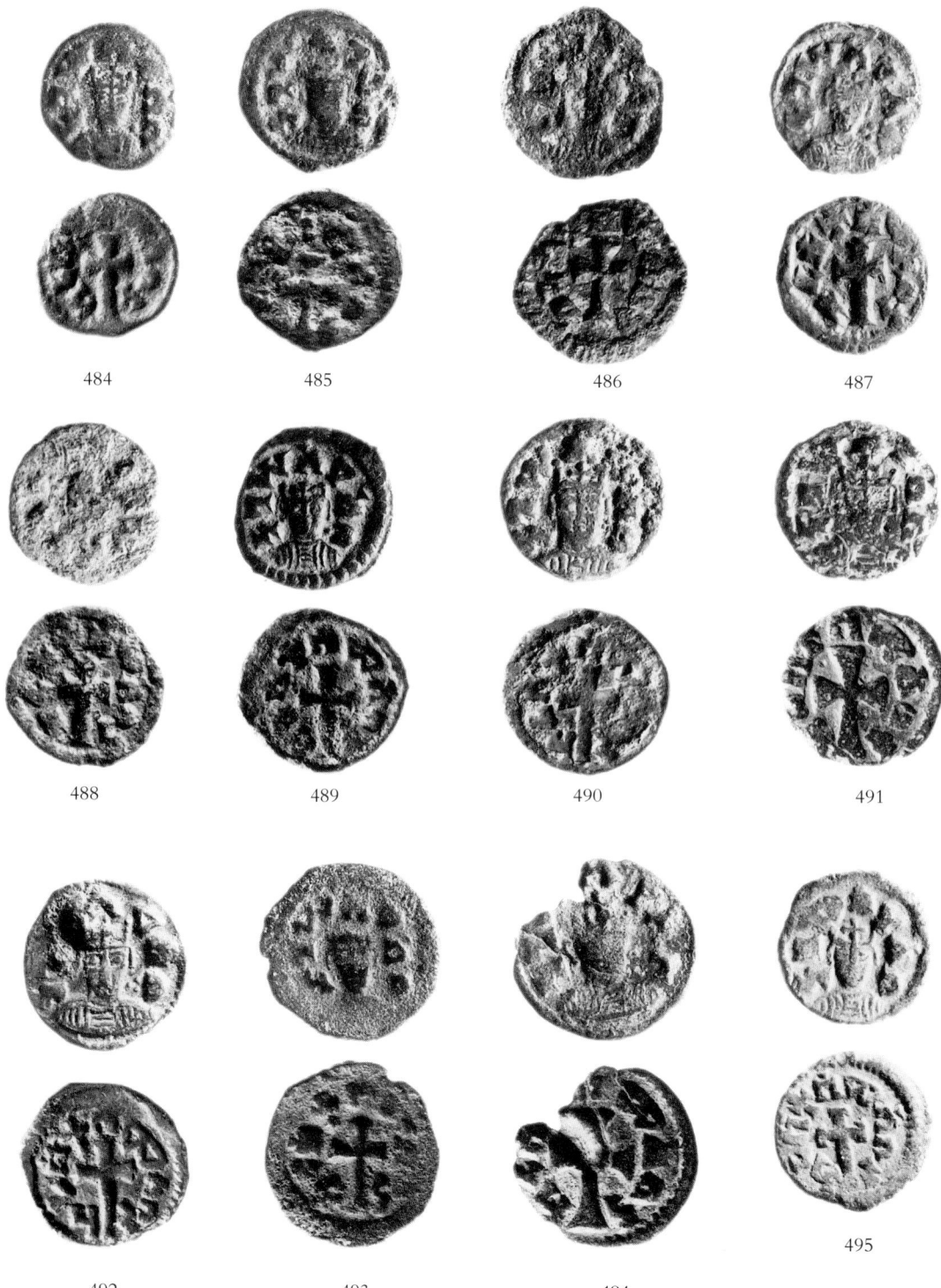

484 485 486 487

488 489 490 491

492 493 494

495

Ioel

PLATE 47

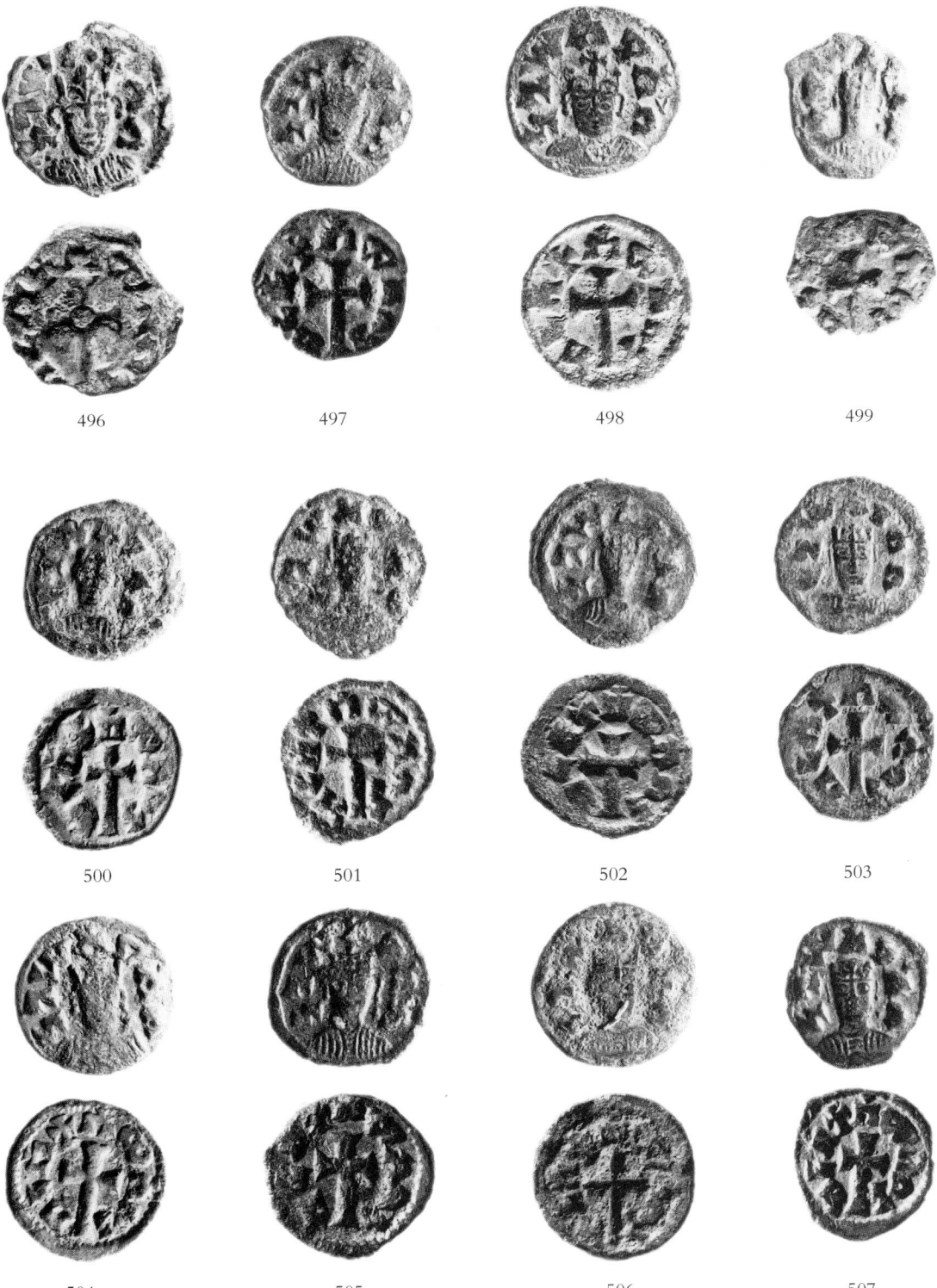

496 497 498 499

500 501 502 503

504 505 506 507

Ioel

PLATE 48

508

509

510

511

512

513

514

515

516

517

518

Ioel (508–14), Ḥataz (515–18)

PLATE 49

519   520

521

523   524   525

522

526   527

Hataz

PLATE 50

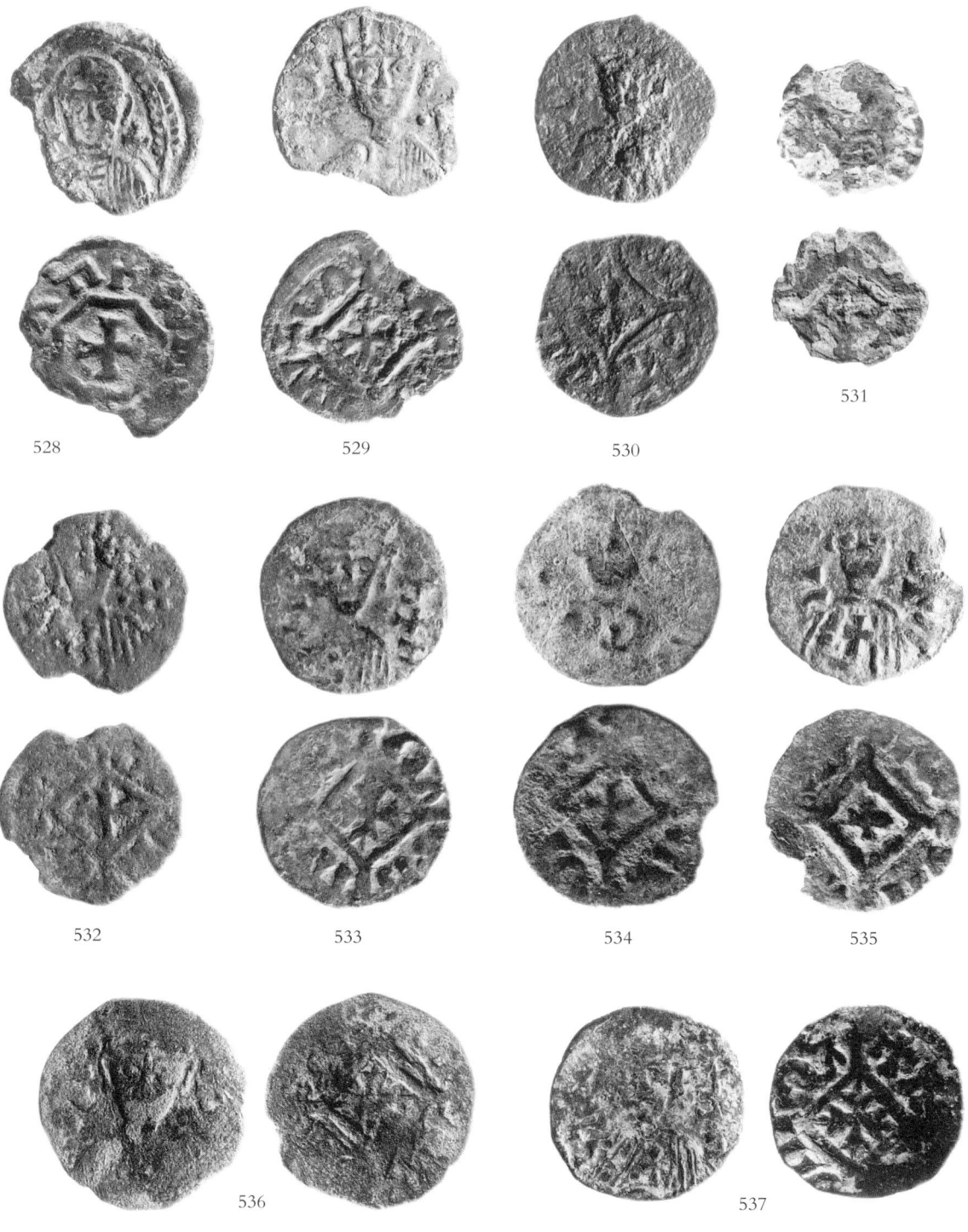

528 529 530 531

532 533 534 535

536 537

Hataz

PLATE 51

538 539 540 541

542 543 544 545

546 547

Hataz

PLATE 52

548 549 550 551

552 553 554 555

556 557

Ḥataz (548–53), Israel (554), Gersem (555–7)

PLATE 53

558 559 560 561

562 563 564 565

566 567

Gersem (558–65), Armaḥ (566–7)

PLATE 54

568

569

570

571

572

573

574

Armaḥ

PLATE 55

575

576

577

578

579

580

Armaḥ

PLATE 56

581

582

583

584

585

586

Armah

PLATE 57

587

588

589

590

591

592

Armah

PLATE 58

593   594   595

596   597   598

Armah

PLATE 59

599

600

601

602

603

604

Armaḥ

PLATE 60

605

606

607

608

609

610

Armah

PLATE 61

611 612 613

614 615 616

Armaḥ

PLATE 62

617 618 619

620 621 622

Armaḥ

PLATE 63

623 624 625

626 627 628

Armaḥ

PLATE 64

a b c d

e f g h

i j k l

Forgeries

PLATE 65

m

n

o

p

q

r

s

v

t

u

Forgeries

PLATE 66

w

x

J-J 191

J-J 79   J-J 404

J-J 192

J-J 193   J-J 396   J-J 194   J-J 112

Forgeries (w–x). Supplementary coins: Aphilas (J-J 191, 79, 404, 192, 193, 396, 194),
Ousanas (J-J 112)

PLATE 67

J-J 403

J-J 308

J-J 152

J-J 64

J-J 154

J-J 251

J-J 300

J-J 247

J-J 196

J-J 384

Supplementary coins: Ousanas (J-J 403, 308, 152), Ezanas (J-J 64, 154), Anonymous
(J-J 251, 300), Mḥdys (J-J 247), Nezana (J-J 196), Anonymous (J-J 384)

PLATE 68

J-J 197   J-J 9   J-J 66   J-J 78

J-J 207   J-J 208   J-J 209   J-J 388

Supplementary coins: Nezool (J-J 197), Ousas (J-J 9, 66), Ousanas (J-J 78, 207),
Kaleb (J-J 208, 209, 388)

PLATE 69

J-J 204

J-J 205

J-J 382

J-J 198

J-J 175

J-J 6

J-J 147

J-J 201

BNF
N 3458 (x1)

Supplementary coins: Kaleb (J-J 204, 205, 382), Ella Amida (J-J 198), Za-ya'abiyo la
mad<u>h</u>en negus (J-J 175), Israel (J-J 6, 147), Gersem (J-J 201), Wazeba (BNF)